STONES FROM THE RIVERBED

Experiencing God's Grace in Mozambique

AMY PARDUE BOONE

Order this book online at www.trafford.com
or email orders@trafford.com

Most Trafford titles are also available at major online book retailers.

Printed in Victoria, BC, Canada.

ISBN: 978-1-4269-1789-9 (sc)

*Our mission is to efficiently provide the world's finest, most comprehensive book publishing
service, enabling every author to experience success. To find out how to publish your book, your
way, and have it available worldwide, visit us online at www.trafford.com*

Trafford rev. 12/07/2009

 www.trafford.com

North America & international
toll-free: 1 888 232 4444 (USA & Canada)
phone: 250 383 6864 ♦ fax: 812 355 4082

DEDICATION

THIS BOOK is dedicated to the godly Pastors in Mozambique that are willing to take the Gospel to the next village, and the next and the next. We honor you, João, and Queraquiwala "Napipi" and Gregoria for the hours you spend on bikes and on foot taking the Gospel to your people. You are our heroes.

To all my other dedicated Mozambican sisters and brothers, thanks for the memories. It won't be long until we hear the trumpet sound and we will be together forever...

It is also dedicated to my dear husband and my two children who have walked this journey with me. Timothy and Grace, you had to follow your parents as we trekked to Africa, and you were troopers. It probably would not have been your decision to come if you would have had the chance to choose. I love all three of you more than words can say. We survived guys.

To Mike's parents and grandparents, I know I married your only son and went with him to Africa and we took your only grandchildren. I know the sacrifice was great for you, and I thank you. I know it was very difficult for you, and I am very mindful of the pain you all went through.

And lastly to my dear parents, James and Judie Pardue. I know many times others have to sacrifice greatly when we follow the will of God. I know it took a heavy toll on you both, as well as on me, when I left. I know you prayed for and worried about everything that will follow in this book. Yet, you never said, "Amy, come home

- it is just too bad." I, though, will always regret that I was away from you for so many years, and couldn't have been more help to you. 'Thank you' seems so inadequate for what you have done - we survived because of your prayers and love.

CONTENTS

PREFACE

W E AS humans are forgetful people. We will remember for years how someone has hurt us, but we will forget tomorrow the good someone did. God knew this about us. That is why he instituted the Lord's Supper, for instance, so that we would always remember His sacrifice. That is why married couples wear rings - to remember the promises made. That is why we give Baptismal certificates - so we can remember that day and the commitment made. Otherwise, we are forgetful people.

Over and over in the Bible, God tells us to remember His goodness. He especially told this to the children of Israel after they were freed from Egypt. He wanted them to remember all He had done for them - how he freed them by His power with the ten plagues, how he saved them from the death angel by the blood on the doorposts, and how he parted the Red Sea. He sustained them in the desert for 40 years - feeding them food that fell from heaven, and giving them water from rocks. Their clothes did not wear out in 40 years, and their feet did not swell after walking for 40 years! They came to a land flourishing with cities they did not build. They had water from wells they did not dig and food from fields they didn't plant. He protected them from the venomous snakes and scorpions in the desert. At times, we wonder how they forgot such huge miracles.

Well, they did, and very quickly. And if I had lived then too, I would have been just like them. When Moses left them for a short time to go to the mountain to receive the Ten Commandments, they decided to forsake their God, and make for themselves a man-made golden god. So I write this as a book of remembrance. You will read about the ten miracles that God did and I pray they will encourage you. But I also write them for myself, that I will never forget what God did. As the patriarchs set up stones as markers of significant events, this is my marker of memories.

"Be careful that you do not forget the Lord, who brought you out of Egypt, out of the land of slavery." Deut. 6:12 "Remember how the Lord your God led you all the way in the desert those forty years." Deut. 8:2a "Be careful that you do not forget the Lord your God, failing to observe his commands, his laws and his decrees that I am giving you this day. Otherwise, when you eat and are satisfied, when you build fine houses and settle down, and when your herds and flocks grow large and your silver and gold increase, then your heart will become proud and you will forget the Lord your God, who brought you out of Egypt, out of the land of slavery. You may say to yourself, 'my power and the strength of my hands have produced this wealth for me.' But remember the Lord your God." Deut. 8: 11-14; 17-18a

"Praise the Lord, O my soul, and forget not all his benefits, who forgives your sins, and heals all your diseases, who redeems your life from the pit and crowns you with love and compassion, who satisfies your desires with good things so that your youth is renewed like the eagles." Psalm 103:2-5

This book is written so I will not forget even one thing He did for us - the way He healed us, gave us compassion, and the strength to endure. To Him be all praise and glory.

This is my story.

*Note- when I refer to the Mozambicans, I will call them 'nationals'. It is more politically correct than saying 'natives'.

MK- is the abbreviation for Missionary Kid

INTRODUCTION

THIS IS a book about our journey as missionaries to Mozambique from the years 1998-2003. It was a journey of faith to survive and even flourish in a war-torn country. Our prayer life deepened as we depended on him for our daily needs. This is a book about many of the joys and hardships we faced. But we faced them all in constant communion with God. We prayed for the rains to come, and then after some floods, we prayed for the rains to stop. We prayed for medicine to be available when we were sick, and for healing. You couldn't just go down to the local drugstore and pick up what you needed. We prayed for safety on washed-out and blown-up bridges. We prayed for help with our language skills so we could correctly say what we needed. We prayed for our crops to grow and flourish and for food to be available at the market. We prayed for our children to grow and be educated in our home in an excellent way. We prayed for protection over our house and our goods in the midst of much crime. Without proper hospitals and pharmacies, cell phones, and towing services, we literally depended on him for our very lives.

We saw God provide in marvelous way for our needs and desires. This book really is about the miracles that God did. In the book of Joshua, we see a great miracle of God. The children of Israel had to cross the Jordan River to get to where God was leading them. There was no other way to get there, except through the river. Their ancestors knew about the crossing of the Red Sea, but to this new generation of Israelites, they had not seen a miracle like this. Joshua tells them to go to the Jordan and stand in it. In other words, they would only see the miracle as they entered the fast moving water. The Jordan River had a very swift current, especially at flood stage. During this time of the year, it could easily be 600 feet wide and 100 feet deep. This was not exactly the time for a crossing. It was large, fast, and powerful. A major obstacle. But this is when God asked them to cross. A million people crossed the river while God pealed the water back like an open curtain.

But before the river resumed its course, 12 men, one from each tribe, were asked a very strange thing indeed. They were asked to go to the middle of the river and pick out 12 stones. Then they were to take them to the other side and build a stone memorial to signify this major event. When they crossed to the other side safely, you can imagine the roar of the water when it resumed its course. A million people could look back and say, "We made it through that?"

The stone memorial was made and Joshua said that it would serve as a testimony to the future generations. It was to be a physical curiousity that was intended to invoke the interest of the next generation. The next generation must be taught the great works of God in the Bible in history, as well as to be taught to see His hand in the midst of life's drudgery today. The next generation does not inherently understand that they live in a world controlled by God's hand. If we fail to pass on what He has done, the next generation will not know.

This book is the same as the 12 stones to me. The contents of this book were taken from the middle of my experience and walk with God in Mozambique. The life lessons that I learned were gained from crossing the river at flood stage. Taking two young children to the poorest country in the world – just emerging from a civil war.

What has God brought you through? When you went through that tragedy, what lessons did you learn in the middle of the storm? God teaches us many times through suffering, learning more than we would have if the storm hadn't of come. The lessons we take out should be remembered. When the next storm comes, we should draw on the strength that we learned from the last trial. This is what I brought out of 28 cases of malaria in my immediate family, 10 robberies, and two car accidents involving pedestrians. I could choose to be bitter, or blessed.

Chapter 1

MY CALLING

I WAS BORN to be a missionary. I knew this from an early age. When I would meet a missionary, and hear his/her stories, I just knew I would be a missionary when I grew up. I grew up in a Christian home, and lived in Germany for three years when I was small. I met missionaries and traveled a lot and saw different cultures and peoples. When I was in the second grade, we had to write a paper about "What I want to be when I grow up". I wrote in that paper that I wanted to be a missionary and tell people about Jesus. My teacher and others who saw that may have just thought that this was a little girl who did not know what she was talking about, and of course, the story would change. But I knew in my heart this was the truth!

I am so grateful for the churches I was involved in and the teaching I received through the years. I am also thankful for the mission's organizations I was involved in as a child and youth. In 1980, my family went to the Baptist World Alliance meeting in Toronto, Canada. Baptists were there from literally all over the world. To see the different colors of people, and different colors of dress intrigued me! I sat next to some Chinese Christians who had come there, but knew that they would be persecuted when they went home. We also met many Africans in their beautiful national outfits and I marveled at them. Each person wore headphones for translation from English to their mother tongue. We met others that had spent their whole savings just to come to this meeting, and did not have enough money to get back home. I was so touched by this meeting. This is what heaven will be like, except that we will not need headphones for translation!

I was privileged to be a preacher's kid, and each year our family vacation would revolve around the Southern Baptist Convention annual meeting. I was fortunate to hear many famous speakers and hear many missionaries. Each year at the convention, they would have an appointment service for new missionaries. The President of the Foreign Mission Board would appeal to the group to try to get new missionaries. At the end of his sermon, he would call for people to respond by coming down to the altar if they were interested in foreign missions. I don't know how many times I went, but it was probably every year! The special flag services would always make me cry. As people in national outfits would march in with the flag of their country, this greatly moved me. In later years, they would carry flags down the aisle that were just grey and had no color or writing. This was to represent the unreached people groups. In my heart, I would cry out, 'I will go to those people who haven't heard'!

I was greatly influenced by my parents. My mother and father always loved internationals. My mother taught sewing and cooking classes to the international women that came to America. Some were refugees, and others were there to study. Many times at Christmas and at other occasions, we would have internationals eating with us. My mother's heart was very tender to them. I can remember having a hard time pronouncing their names, but I will never forget the love my parents had for them.

My father too was involved in ministering to them. At three out of the six churches he pastored, he allowed the building to be used for other language groups. For instance, in Memphis, there was a huge group of Laotians that had settled there, and later Hispanics. He enlisted pastors for these groups and would then plant a church that would meet simultaneously with our worship service, just in a different part of the building. In the Laotian church, many of them were trying to learn English. I played the piano for their services, and I became burdened that they didn't know many English songs. I photocopied about 50 easy English hymns and choruses and printed them in a little spiralbound book and they used that as their hymnbook for years. I did this while in high school!

I was also fortunate to go to a large church that had full-time Youth ministers and Music ministers. They would organize annual camps and at those camps, missions was also emphasized. We also went on annual choir tours and mission trips. Near Memphis, many Hispanic migrants had settled. Our youth group would go there and lead Vacation Bible Schools each summer and I lived for those times.   In the other churches Dad pastored, I also got involved in the Hispanic ministry.

My family lived in Memphis, Tennessee for 11 years. I was there from fourth grade until I was a sophomore in college. During these years, racial tension was very high - these were the Civil Rights years. When I was about to enter Middle School for Sixth Grade, they began bussing children from one area to another, to make for racial equality. I was bussed to a school about 30 minutes away that was 85% African-American. Our church was in the inner-city and the community was very racially mixed, and we had a few African-Americans in my youth group. It was of course in this very city, that Martin Luther King was assassinated. In my high school, I can remember a racial riot, when a group of black and white students began to attack one another, and I was pushed under a desk by a friend to avoid being hurt. We also had many bomb threats because of these issues. Racial tensions were very high, yet this was a perfect environment for me to grow and learn. Although a child, I remember being deeply affected by this, and it instilled in me the desire for racial equality.

When we first moved to this city, our house was not ready for us to move into it. A single lady in the church opened up her home for us to live for several weeks. She was a retired missionary from China. I can remember all the beautiful pearl-inlaid chests from China, and the other artifacts and curios. I remember her telling us story after story of her life in China. All of this contributed to my call!

When I went to college, I choose Samford University, a Baptist university. Because we had lived in Germany for a while as a child, I was classified as a 'missionary kid'. I really didn't qualify to be on this list, as we were only there for three years, and my parents were not with the mission board, but were rather the pastor of a church. But I really feel it was the providence of God that I got on this list! This group of missionary children was under the care of a professor, who was a former missionary to Nigeria. He would get the group together often for cook-outs and if people needed a place to stay during the holidays, he arranged for that also. He also arranged regular care packages for us! I felt quite spoiled, because my parents were fairly close by, while many of these missionary kids had parents overseas. I learned so much about missionary life from fellowshipping with this group!

During my university days, and then later in seminary, we had a certain amount of chapel services that we were required to go to each semester. During many of these services, they would have missionary speakers. I am sure they did not know the impact they were having on this young woman! I can remember them using the story of the popular chorus "Kum by Yah"- translated, it means "come by here". This was a song that was sung by Africans as they petitioned the missionaries to please come to them. They were in a remote area, and the traveling missionaries could only come rarely, as they had many other places to visit as well. The other verses are "Someone's crying, come by here", and "Someone's praying, come by here." I can remember sitting in those beautiful chapels and hearing those stories, and I would say to God, "I will go!"

In 1984, I went to Nigeria with a group from my university. I was so excited to be finally going to Africa! I had met Africans and heard missionaries from Africa speak, but this was my first chance to go there. The night before we were to go, the country went through a government *coup d'etat*. When we got there, there were soldiers with guns everywhere. I have never seen so many guns in my whole life.

We had many experiences while we were there for the two weeks. For part of the time, we stayed in a university dorm and worked with the college ministry. One of the first things my Nigerian roommate told me was that she got up at four a.m. each morning to pray. She said the university, since it was in the north of the country, was mostly comprised of Muslim students. The Christians on campus were persecuted and ridiculed. She said she had to wake up at 4:00 each day to pray for several hours for God to give her the strength to make it through that day as a Christian on that Muslim campus. Her dedication was so inspiring. Her church had been burned down by the Muslims, as had many other churches.

At one church we went to in the south, there were 3,000 Nigerians in attendance- all in their beautiful, colorful clothes. I was so moved by their worship. During the prayer and testimony time, different people would come up to share prayer requests. One was a man and he had found out that week that he needed glasses. But he did not have the money to buy them. So he took his request to the church, and all 3,000 people prayed out loud at once for him to be able to buy glasses. I was so moved by this demonstration of faith. To me, when I find out I need glasses, I just go and buy them. Here was a man, and a people, that had to pray about their needs, and they lived by faith.

I was so moved by the beautiful African people, the African sunsets, and all the flowering trees and plants. It is a beauty that you can't describe. At the end of my trip, I got very ill and had to be hospitalized. I was in and out of consciousness, but at one time a group of volunteer missionaries from Alabama came to visit me. They had heard about this Alabama college student that was in the hospital. They came and prayed for me, and I saw that God is so powerful. It is a small world! I was sick up until the very end of our trip, and had to be taken to the airplane in a wheelchair. But as I got on that plane, I knew that one day I would come and live on this continent. I would only arrive back in Africa after 13 years from my first trip, but I knew God had called me to this place.

Keith Green was a popular singer at the time. He wrote many pamplets and then a book about missions. I got to hear him in concert one time. His main statement was that if God has not called you to stay, you are called to go. I said, "Lord, I will go!"

Throughout my life, God continued to solidify this call. I knew in my heart I would be a missionary. I evaluated everything I did by this future calling- my choice of majors, how I spent my time, and who I dated. For instance, while in Birmingham, Alabama at college, I joined a lovely, large Southern Baptist church. They had an orchestra and a great music program, which was right up my alley since I was a cellist and majoring in music. But as I sat in those warm, comfortable pews, I began to know that this was not where I needed to be. Our college Sunday School class had hundreds of students in the class, and I was just one of many. I really wanted to make a difference in my world, and just couldn't sit in a comfortable church! So I found a juvenile prison, called

Family Court, and called the chaplain. I asked him if they needed any help on Sundays with their service. He was so thrilled to meet my friend and me. We went each Sunday and led the music and led a small choir of the prisoners. I even wrote an Easter play, and inserted songs in to it, to make an Easter musical that the prisoners performed in front of everyone. I knew this was where I belonged on Sundays!

I majored in voice, because I so wanted to sing for the Lord. But the only kind of music they offered was classical voice training. So I was immediately learning arias in French, Italian and other languages. My teacher forbade me to sing any popular Christian songs, like by Amy Grant, saying that when I would sing that style, I would revert back to my incorrect style of singing that I did before I started taking classes from her. She told me that during my training with her, for four years, I could not sing in any church on Sundays. So one Monday during my class, I was not doing very well in the classical style. She asked me what I had done on the day previously. I told her I had sung a solo in church. She slapped me! I have never forgotten that day. How I continued to study with her and get a four-year voice degree is only by the grace of God. But to me, I knew I would never sing that kind of music on the mission field, and it seemed like such a waste of time! But now, as I have matured, I see what she was trying to do, but it didn't make sense then.

My call to missions also determined whom I dated! I only wanted to date guys that were interested in missions. If they didn't want to be a missionary, I knew they weren't for me. But one day, I did fall in love with a young man that wanted to be in the ministry in America. He had never had an interest in missions. When he was called to the ministry, he was advised by an older pastor that if you are called to the ministry, that is synonymous to being called to preach. At that time, they didn't know about all the different types of missionaries there were, and all the different types of ministers. For instance, many people are involved in coaching and playing sports, and they become sports evangelists. That is just as worthy a profession as a preacher. But in that day and time, that was the advice he got. (As he looks back on it, if someone would have told him about agricultural missions, he knows that would have been the route he took!) I was deeply in love with him, but didn't know what I was going to do with this call of God. After we had dated for over a year, he took me to a lovely, expensive restaurant overlooking Birmingham. As we were eating, he took out a little box and asked me to marry him! And I hated to do it, but I said " no". He was so rejected - it made for a very quiet ride home in the car!

This sweet, patient man is now my husband of 20 years. The Lord told me that in His time, He would work out my love for Mike and my call to missions. We did get married, and after we were married, God called him to missions. We have now been on the mission field for 11 years.

Chapter 2

PREPARING FOR MISSIONS

IKE AND I were pastoring a church in Salemburg, North Carolina. We were very happy there, but God began to put on Mike's heart that He had something else for us. Mike grew up on a farm and loves agriculture and being outside. One day, while Mike was a pastor, we went to hear an Agricultural Missionary speak at a Missions Banquet. That night, while that man spoke, Mike knew that was what he was put on this earth to do! He immediately realized that he would have to resign and go back to college full-time to get an agricultural degree. This seemed crazy for a 30 year old, with two kids, to resign from his job, and go back to get a bachelor's degree, after already having another bachelor's degree and a Master's degree. Just to ease into the studying and to see if this was really what God had for us, Mike began to take a few courses at the community college at night. He did it for a while, without telling the church, and then after a while, we announced to the church our desire to be foreign missionaries. They gave us their blessing and allowed Mike to drive to North Carolina State University in Raleigh one day a week for classes and also to study at night. As he got into his agricultural classes, the Lord confirmed that this was His will.

But financially we didn't know how we would make it. In the pastorate, along with our salary, they provided a lovely four-bedroom home, medical insurance, and retirement. The church employed me as the youth minister, so I also drew a part-time salary. We would have to leave all of this, plus have money for tuition, which is not cheap. Mike applied for a scholarship and we waited to see what would happen. He did not get it, and had to pay for his first semester.

I began to get deeply worried about how we would live and where we would live. Mike applied for a job at a demonstration farm in the Agricultural department, and he got it, but it was just 20 hours a week at minimum wage - about $150.00 a week. We also began to look for an apartment, looking at many apartments for rent. Some of the cheaper ones were in rough areas, and we felt it would not be safe there. We finally found one of the cheapest ones, and it was $800.00 a month. To me, I couldn't see how God was going to work all this out.

I have terrible migraines, and have suffered with them since high school. One day, as I was worrying about how we would afford to live while Mike studied, I got a migraine. It was so bad that I had to be rushed to the hospital. I was vomiting so much and was in such pain. A lovely deacon from our church in Salemburg was a nurse at the hospital. He was working in the emergency room the night that I was admitted. He oversaw my case, and they gave me a shot of the strongest pain medicine available in a huge dose. But it did not help at all. He came to me and said he had never seen anyone that didn't react positively to that strong medicine. I of course couldn't tell him about all the fear and pain I was feeling about the future, because at that time, we hadn't resigned yet. We were doing all these things, such as looking for apartments, without the church knowing about it. Finally, after several treatments, the migraine did go away, but the deacon from our church just couldn't understand why I was in such pain and so stressed. (After we resigned, I told him the story, and he understood!)

I was willing to go to work to support Mike while he went to school, but I was hesitant about putting my two small children in daycare. Timothy was three and Grace was six months old. I had enjoyed up to now staying home with them. I know many women do have to put their kids in a daycare, and I knew I would have to, but it was going to be hard. So I began applying for a job. The night I got out of the hospital, I got a call from Dr. Ray Campbell - the head of the Minister of Music search committee from Ephesus Baptist Church in Raleigh. They needed a part-time Minister of

Music and this was just perfect for me, since I also wanted to be with my children.

We started the long process of interviews and meetings. I went up and sang and played the piano for them. They felt that they wanted me to come, and they wanted to discuss my salary and benefits. By this time, the cheapest apartment in a nicer area we could find was the one for $800.00 a month. The committee wanted to know how much we felt we needed each month, and they would base the salary on that. I told them I didn't feel like it was right for me to "name the price". I did have a figure in mind, but wanted them to offer first! If we needed to negotiate later, that was fine, but I did not feel right telling them what to pay me. We had added up the rent, daycare, utilities and other bills, and came up with a figure in our mind. When they told me later what they were willing to pay, it was *EXACTLY* the dollar amount that we had come up with!! God just confirmed over and over that this was the place I was to serve. Another time on the phone with Dr. Campbell, when he was telling me more about the job, he told me that the church had a preschool and that I could leave Timothy and Grace in the preschool while I worked; that they would be just down the hall from me! (The interesting fact is that just a year or two after we left Ephesus for the mission field, they stopped having a preschool. So it was in operation just for a few years, and God allowed it to be there while I was on staff!!)

With many tears, we did resign from the pastorate and move to Raleigh. We had to get rid of lots of furniture to downsize from our four-bedroom house with a full den and living room to live in an apartment. Mike had made a big jungle gym in the backyard of the parsonage. We had to leave it behind at the parsonage when we moved to Raleigh. The first week I was at work in the church in Raleigh, I heard them talking about having a workday the following Saturday to build a playground for the preschool! I told them about the jungle gym we had left at the parsonage, just two hours away, if they would be willing to get a big truck and go and move it. They did, and so our children even got to play on their *own* jungle gym everyday at the preschool. God was so good to provide this, since at the apartment, we had no yard, after having such a huge yard at the parsonage.

When we first moved to Raleigh, Grace was six months old, and was too young to go to the church preschool, as it started only at two years old. I tried and tried to find someone to keep her, but just never felt good about it. Most of the daycares were for a full day, and I only needed it part-time. I tried to find a lady to keep her, but nothing was working out. One day as I was particularly worried about it, the Lord spoke so clearly to me. He reminded me of the story of Moses, and how God cared for him while he was in the basket, floating down the Nile River and allowed him to escape harm and be raised in the palace, with his own mother to nurse him. He clearly said to me, that if He could care for baby Moses, He could care for Grace. After that, I put her in God's hands, and He did provide a lady to keep her until she was old enough to come with me to the church's preschool!

Our three years at Ephesus were such a blessing. We had a wonderful ministry, and felt such love from the people. Mike did get his degree in three years while I was at the church. He did pay for the first semester, but after that, he got a full scholarship for the next 2 ½ years. In his last year, he even got an extra $1,000 to buy books, or it could even be used to pay rent. God was so good to us. Mike did work at the experimental farm and learned so much, but eventually had to quit to make more money, as we were not making ends meet. That $800.00 rent bill each month was such a concern. We literally did not see how we were going to make it each month. Mike began to be a self-employed painter. He would get a job that would last for two weeks, and then I would get so worried, because he wouldn't have anything lined up after that house. But that person would tell another person, and for the next two years, he was never without work, not even for a day. Many times I would go to a staff meeting, and tell the staff to please pray for us, that Mike had no job after the present job. Then a week later at the next staff meeting, they would ask me how it was going, and to my embarrassment, I would tell them that he had just gotten a call in the nick of time!

Chapter 3

CHOOSING MOZAMBIQUE

A s our three years were winding to a close, and Mike was about to graduate, it was time for us to finalize our appointment with the International Mission Board. We had done all the paperwork, and now it was time for us to pick the country we felt called to. At that time, there were only six jobs open for an Agricultural Evangelist. As we read each of them, and prayed, we had no idea which one to choose. They were all places we had never been to, and most of them, never heard of! So Mike decided that we would pray for a month separately over these six places, and after the month we would come together and say which one we felt called to. During that month of praying and research, God put the country of Mozambique so much on our heart. After the month, Mike said "Mozambique" and I did too! We informed the board and they made all the final preparations for our appointment and departure.

When this was all happening in 1996-1997, e-mail was becoming popular. We got so excited whenever we got e-mails from missionaries in Mozambique. It just confirmed our call. We asked them a trillion questions about what to bring, and what we would eat, and where we would live, etc. Each time we turned on our computer and had an e-mail all the way from Mozambique; I can't describe the feeling! We just knew this was where we were to spend the rest of our lives.

But as we began to research more about the country, and as we received responses to our questions, we began to get very concerned. Mozambique was the poorest country in the world at that time - having come out of a brutal civil war only a few years past. There were still two million land mines underground. Malaria was rampant, and medical care was scarce. We would read the newsletters from the missionaries there, about the crime and their sicknesses and all our excitement soon died! One day, we were about to tell the mission board we just couldn't go. As a painter, Mike always left the house about 7:00 a.m. to begin his work. He would try to get a few hours of work in before he had classes, and sometimes in the summer, he would paint early to avoid the hottest part of the day. On this day, the owner of the house only wanted him to come at 10:00, so he was at home until then, which was very rare. He was always gone by 7:00 to try to earn as much money as possible, since he was self-employed! I too always went to the church early, but didn't feel well, and was also at home that morning. Before long, the phone rang. It was David Hooten, the mission administrator from Mozambique. A real phone call from Mozambique from this person we had been e-mailing! The connection was as clear as a bell - as if he was calling from next door. He called to talk with us personally about the fears we were having. We talked for almost an hour. There are several miracles in this. First of all, we were not ever home at that time. Secondly, usually the connection is so poor due to the weak phone lines. And third, this phone call was costing him a fortune, but he just kept talking to us about our fears and our call. After that phone call, we felt the presence of God in such a clear way. It was as if God was saying, "It is going to be okay."

But again, I began to worry. If it was just Mike and I, I would have been fine. But I was taking two small children over there. Would I be able to home school them? Would I survive being away from my dear parents? Could we learn the language? Were we going to be safe from malaria and land mines? Three times, I had to be rushed to the emergency room. This time, it wasn't headaches, but I began to have heart pains, with my arms going numb. I just knew I was having a heart attack! Finally after the third visit to the emergency room, and all the tests, the doctor told me that I was having panic attacks, and that it was stress. Now if there was ever a person called to missions, it was me! And if there was a couple ever specifically called to a specific place, it was us to

Mozambique. But all this head knowledge did not ease the pain in my heart of leaving my family and my home and going to a place I didn't know.

I mention all of these personal experiences, such as these three hospital visits, and the other hospital visit when I had the migraine that wouldn't go away, to show how difficult it was for me to think of leaving. Many times, people put missionaries on a pedestal. People may think that they could never be a missionary because it would hurt too badly for them to leave, and that the missionaries are over there because it was easy for them. We are real people, with real pain, and we must all be obedient to the call of God - no matter the price.

About that time, we got some photographs of the city of Mocuba. Some missionaries had been there and took many pictures of some of the houses, the Catholic cathedral, and some of the schools and public buildings. They went into one of the little cafes, and took a picture of the white plastic tables, red checkered tablecloths, and Cokes on the tables. To those of you that know me, you will know I am a Coke freak! As soon as I saw the picture of the Cokes, God just reassured in my heart that everything was going to be fine! It is funny what God uses to reassure us.

We also heard from them that the people from the Baptist Church in Mocuba had been praying for years for this request to be filled. They so wanted a missionary in their city. (The closest missionary was two hours away from them). So to hear how badly we were wanted and needed helped so much.

We began to make our decision public and were commissioned at First Baptist Church in Dallas in September of 1997. We are very grateful to our family and friends that came to this special service. My family had a special commissioning service for us and we took the Lord's Supper together. I will never forget what they did to promise their prayer support. They gave us a clock drawn on a sheet of paper. They had each chosen a time in the day when they would pray for us. They then put their name beside the hour on the clock. It was one of the nicest gifts we received during this send-off time. It was such a comfort to know they would pray for us all during the day and night. We felt so blessed and so covered in prayer.

Ephesus sent us off in style and with so much love. We knew of their deep commitment to pray for us and to send out our newsletter and to send packages and anything else we needed. They gave us a huge send-off, and gave us furniture and commissioned us as well. Also at this time, we needed to crate our goods to send to Africa. To come to Africa, your appliances have to be 220 volts, not 110 like the American appliances. So we had to have a new freezer, refrigerator, washer and dryer, and all the small appliances. We also had to buy a 3-4 years supply of so many things: contact solution, clothes and toys for the kids, school books, toiletries, medicines, feminine and food products, etc.

We will always be grateful for the many people that helped us in this time. I will never be able to thank the Ephesus church enough for the money they gave us to buy all those things. It was a huge miracle. Many other Baptist churches also contributed to the list of supplies we needed. One church, Salem Baptist in Apex, NC, got all their children's mission classes to bring toys for Timothy and Grace. I wanted to have some toys put up, so that at every birthday and Christmas, they would get something special from America. When we left America, Timothy was six and Grace three. They planned it out to give us age-appropriate toys for Timothy when he would be ages seven, eight, and then nine and the same for Grace!

One had to be quite an astute packer to fit all the things in we felt we would need. We took the back off the couch, and crammed toilet paper rolls and many other things in that empty space. We also took the fabric off the bottom of the box springs and put all kinds of things in the box springs. We filled the washer tub and the dryer with food items. We found things hidden even months after we unpacked the shipping container! Ten years later, we are still using some of the things we bought 11 years ago! It is hard to calculate how much deodorant one will need, but we are still using those deodorant sticks we packed so long ago!

One of my main concerns was about what we would eat! We knew that groceries were limited, and I really did wonder what in the world I would fix my family. We got advice from other missionaries on things we should bring. The strangest thing we did was can hamburger meat! I remember buying 50 lbs. of hamburger meat and canning it on Mike's grandmother's porch. If all else failed, I could make spaghetti and other familiar things with it. We did use it, but I must admit, canned hamburger meat is not good!

As we prepared to go, we got all the usual questions- "Are you taking your children with you?" " How long will you stay?", etc. When they would ask us about our children - we got asked it so many times - that we tried to think of funny answers so they would see how crazy that question was! We would tell them that we were going to leave them behind in our apartment and just leave them with enough food and water to last for four years!

Many people did not know what to say to us. Almost everyone thought we were crazy. Few people said to us that they were so happy for us, and just knew we would be fine, etc. One person said to us that they were upset because we were going to go over there and live with those n*****s; I hate that word! Another person, said something so hurtful, I have never forgotten it. We were sharing with a church about Mozambique and how the war just ended and that people were so hungry for the Gospel. We were so excited as we showed the slides we had been sent from missionaries that had been to where we would live in Mozambique. The church we were at was a church where my father had been a pastor. It had been a few years since my father had gone to another church, but many in that church still loved my parents. A man came to me, after our slide presentation, and said this to me, " I didn't know your father raised a fool." He said that if I took my children there, I was the worst mother ever. I have never forgotten that statement, or the pain it caused for months to come, as Satan used that comment to make me feel that I was making a huge mistake.

I am thankful for one positive comment I got from my uncle. After hearing all about our future country and work, he told me that because I had one of the most positive attitudes he had ever seen; he just knew we were going to love it. He said your attitude will make or break you - and he was right!

Little Grace, age three, just wanted to know if we were going to turn black when we moved to Africa!

We then went to Richmond, Virginia to begin an eight-week orientation. While there, the anxiety and fear grew stronger and stronger. I had to go to counseling, because the fear of the future was debilitating me. After listening to my story, the counselor said some very wise words. He said that I had the "chicken little" disease. Chicken Little is a timeless classic children's book. At the start of the book, an acorn fell from an oak tree and hit her on the head. She began to tell everyone that the sky was falling – starting a chain reaction of panic. At the end of the book she discovers that it was just an acorn that fell from the tree. She plants the acorn and later it grows into a huge oak tree – that her grandchildren snuggle under to hear her story. The counselor told me I was expecting the worst in Mozambique. He told me that half the things I was worried about would not come true. It was advice that I still use today, because I still have the "chicken little" disease. It goes in remission in the times when I trust in God, but in other times, I can feel that the sky is falling.

The greatest fear that I had when I was leaving was that someone in our family would die while we were overseas. When you say goodbye, you never know if that will be the last time you see them. I really became obsessed with that thought, and had to go to counseling. Although it is better, it still haunts me everytime I leave.

In times like this, I had to really believe the promises from His Word. Verses that were particularly meaningful to me at this time were:

"And everyone who has left houses or brothers or sisters or father or mother or children or fields for my sake will receive a hundred times as much and will inherit eternal life." Matthew 19:29

"Anyone who loves his father or mother more than me is not worthy of me; anyone who loves his son or daughter more than me is not worthy of me; and anyone who does not take his cross and follow me is not worthy of me. Whoever finds his life will lose it, and whoever loses his life for my sake will find it." Matthew 10:37-39

We literally clung to them as we left!

Chapter 4

A LITTLE ABOUT MOZAMBIQUE

P EOPLE HAVE lived in Mozambique since the days before
Christ, so historians say. The Arabs moved there in the 800's.
The Portuguese explorers first visited Mozambique in 1497
and established it as a trading post, and a slave-trading center.
In 1885, Africa was divided among various European powers and
Mozambique was recognized as a Portuguese colony. It was at that
time called Portuguese East Africa.

Towns and railways were built up, and by the early 1900's the
white Portuguese population grew. In the 1950's, many of the
Mozambicans became increasingly discontent with the white
Portuguese rule. A guerilla movement called Frelimo, began
military attacks against the Portuguese in 1964. A brutal war
ensued between Frelimo and the white Portuguese for 10 years.
During this time, the 600,000 Portuguese were forced to leave.
Their houses and cars and possessions were confiscated, and they
were forced to leave with only one suitcase each. These people
had many developments in this country - resorts, hotels and
businesses - and they left with only one suitcase. Everything they
had worked for became fair game. Houses, restaurants, and hotels
were immediately "claimed" by squatters. Many told us the story
of how, when the Portuguese were forced to leave the country,
they sabotaged the Mozambicans to deny them the privilege of
using what they had built and had to leave behind. An example
of these acts was the Portuguese filling a drainage system with
concrete so that the hotel would be rendered useless. Another was

destroying the rail lines, so that the Mozambicans could not export their crops.

Although it is very sad what happened to the Portuguese people, in a way they reaped what they sowed. Many of them were very unkind to the Mozambican people. (There are always many exceptions of Portuguese that genuinely loved the people and did many things to help them.) As a whole though, the Portuguese colonized the country primarily for what they could get out of it - mainly all the natural resources and goods to export. While this is true of most European countries that colonized Africa, some of the other colonial powers also tried to develop the country for the sake of the people. This is seen in many of the British colonies. But if schools and clinics were built in Mozambique, they were built mostly to benefit only the Portuguese and those in the cities.

We heard many tales about the Portuguese while we lived there. The Mozambicans would tell how there were curfews and how the Portuguese made them get off the streets at a certain time each night. The Mozambicans told us how when they were walking on the sidewalk, and were passed by a Portuguese, they had to get off the sidewalk and walk in the road. They sent many of the Mozambican males to work in South Africa and Rhodesia (now Zimbabwe), thus removing a large portion of the male labor force. Cash crops were then introduced in Mozambique and all men over 15 years of age had to work on the plantations for six months of every year for a minimal wage. Laborers were often chained.

Mozambique became independent in 1975 after this war with the Portuguese. The Frelimo government took control. It was a government based on the policies of the philosophers Karl Marx and Lenin - thus being run on Communist principles. After independence, a brutal civil war ensued for the next 16 years.

In 1984, another party was formed, called Renamo - the National Resistance Movement. They were not happy with how Frelimo was running the country. This terrible 16-year civil war disrupted farming and other economic activities. Along with famines and droughts, millions of people starved to death due to the war and natural disasters.

Renamo was established by the neighboring countries of Rhodesia and South Africa, who were both controlled by white governments. Their aim was the wholesale destruction of the social and communication infrastructure within Mozambique and thus the destabilization of the government and the country. They wanted to bring Mozambique to its knees to force them to allow the Portuguese to continue to rule. In trying to destroy the country, roads, bridges, railways, school and clinics were destroyed. Atrocities were committed on a massive and horrific scale. Villagers were rounded up and anyone with skills - teachers, medical workers, etc. – were shot. At the end of the war, it was reported that 900 shops, 495 primary schools, 86 health posts, and 140 villages had been destroyed.

Finally in 1990, talks began between Frelimo and Renamo and a peace treaty was signed in 1992. In 1994, the first multi-party elections were held. But twenty years of such brutal wars had taken its toll. Two million land mines were still underground; one million people were dead. There were three million refugees, and the economy and rail lines were destroyed. When we moved there in 1998, we saw the catastrophic effects of the war: blown up buildings, and buildings full of bullet holes. We saw tanks in the streets and derailed trains that had been destroyed. The total infrastructure was in shambles. But the best thing was that people were tired of war after 20 years, and most were eager to rebuild their country.

We heard so many tales of the war. Many people fled to the forest with their possessions and livestock and did not emerge until after the civil war ended. When the war ended, and they did come out from the forest, they were found dressed in tree bark. Food was scarce and many died of hunger. The war was very brutal, with drunken soldiers coming into the villages and raping the women, and even cutting off their noses and breasts. It was also very common to see people who had had their legs blown off by the land mines. During the war the boys could go to school, when possible, but the girls were never allowed to be educated.

It is no wonder the Portuguese settled in Mozambique. The 2,500-kilometer coastline is known for some of the most beautiful beaches in the world. The shrimp and lobsters are renowned, as well as many beautiful tropical fish that are only found in these waters. Tourists from all over the world go there to snorkel, boat and fish. There are some beautiful beach resorts only for the very rich. Sugar, cotton and cashews are grown in abundance and became major money-making exports. There is an Archipelago made up of 32 offshore coral islands. A rich South African businessman just bought one of the islands for $20 million. The beauty is very difficult to describe.

Although known for its beauty, it is also known for the natural disasters that occur there. A cyclone came in 2000, and killed hundreds and displaced a million people. In 2001, flooding came and killed tens of thousands and left as many homeless. This is the flooding that was announced all over the world, as a lady gave birth in a tree, while trying to escape the raging waters below. In 2003, heavy rains came again and left 100,000 families homeless and severely damaged crops, roads and bridges. In 2006, another cyclone came that totally wiped away a whole city. Droughts are also common. Whether it is too much rain, or not enough, all of this leads to starvation.

In many ways, most of the people continue to live like other ancient civilizations. They still make dug-out canoes out of trees. They grow most all their own food, cut down fire wood to cook, and they have to go to the river or public tap to draw water to cook and bathe. The women and girls spend many hours a day walking to the well or river, waiting in line to get water, and then walking home with it, a bucket at a time on their head. Most don't have refrigeration or electricity. In many ways the people just survive from day to day. They spend their whole day just getting enough wood and water to cook their food and care for their families. The life expectancy is 40, and with this hard life, a 40 year old woman will look like she is 60. Old people are greatly revered because there are so few of them. Life is a daily struggle just to survive.

When we moved there it was known as the poorest country in Africa, as well as the country with the greatest amount of human needs - like health care and clean water. The effects of malaria are great, killing millions each year. It is ranked among the ten nations most affected by this disease. They make an average of $80 per year; that is $1.50 per week. Only 37% have a chance of going to school.

It was to this country that we were called. The people were very receptive to the Gospel as many had lost so much in the war. The harvest was ripe and we couldn't have been more excited to be going there.

Chapter 5

LEAVING FOR AFRICA

W E LEFT America in January 1998, with a deep call in our
hearts, but with great sorrow as we left our families. I
literally felt my heart would break as I said goodbye
to my parents. I knew I would see them in 2 years, but it seemed
like an eternity. Mike is an only child, and I felt so guilty about
leaving his family, and taking their only grandchildren (and great
grandchildren).

We arrived in Africa in the country of Zimbabwe. It was the
closest international airport to where we would be living. Plus,
other missionaries wanted us to stock up on food and meat. At that
time, Zimbabwe had very nice stores and butcheries. When we
arrived at the airport, they parked the plane far from the airport,
and there was no covered walkway to get inside the airport. As
we got off the plane, we began to see the small group of four
missionaries that were there to meet us. I can still remember
their hearty waves from the second floor balcony! As we entered
the airport, we first had to present an entry form to the passport
control center and have our passports stamped. Well, I didn't have
a pen, and just thought I would fill out the form when I got up to
the man at the counter. The line was so long, and we were all so
tired, having just flown for two days! When I finally got to the
front of the line, I asked the man for a pen. He yelled at me and
said, "Go find a pen and move to the back of the line." I was
about in tears!! I would have thought that the nice African man
would have realized the trauma I had just been through, having

left my parents, and he would have said, "Welcome to Africa. It is so wonderful that you have come here to help us!" But I got yelled at instead. This would be the first of many times when things didn't live up to my expectations. One of the missionaries that met us was David Hooten – the man that called us that day in North Carolina when we were trying to decide whether we should come. He would later drive us into Mozambique. We will never forget his kindness to us.

The night before we were to enter Mozambique, we got some very wonderful words from a fellow missionary. He told us that, as we traveled the eight hours to Mozambique, we should try to see the people on the side of the road, through the eyes of the Lord. We must see them as God sees them - " as sheep without a shepherd." Of all the advice we got, this has stuck with me the most. During the difficult days, when we really didn't feel like we loved the people, we clung to this advice. Still to this day, I try to see the masses as God sees them - to not grow cold when seeing poverty and need - but to always view them through the eyes of God. This was deeply meaningful to us.

We began immediately to realize we were really in a foreign country. We left Zimbabwe, after flying there from America, and drove eight hours to Beira, Mozambique. Beira, a city of 500,000, is a port city on the Indian Ocean. We knew a cyclone had just hit Mozambique, so we were fearful of what that would mean on our trip, as well as what effects we would find when we arrived. Also due to political unrest, riots broke out in Zimbabwe the day after we left. It made the international news in America, and our families saw the riots and assumed we were still in Zimbabwe, but we had left the day earlier!

During our eight-hour trip, we passed from Harare, the capital, to another city called Mutare. It is a very crowded city, and when you would pull up to a traffic light, people were begging and looking in your windows. Timothy had been pretty quiet up until now, but the masses of people, and those begging really began to bother him as we drove. Our car was so loaded down with the eight trunks we had brought with us, that one of us had to stand guard, while the rest of us went in to eat lunch. One little boy in particular latched on to us. He followed us from our car to the restaurant, and then peered at us through the restaurant window.

When we finished lunch and returned to our car, he followed us to the car - all the time asking for money and rubbing his stomach like he was hungry. He then pressed his face against the glass - such a scary sight. The experienced missionary with us had told us it is best not to give to these beggars - that they must go to school. When you give them money, it makes them want to stay on the streets. So we kept refusing to give him money, since that is what we had been advised. The whole trip, Timothy was fairly shell-shocked and traumatized and he kept his head in his little Game Boy. But when that boy kept following us, he yelled at us to give him some money or food. He, even as a six-year-old boy, began crying about this first beggar. He was immediately deeply touched by this young boy. It would be the first of hundreds of beggars that one does not know how to handle. We could see from the reaction of Timothy, and the way he broke down, that we were all in shambles emotionally.

We then got to the border post between Zimbabwe and Mozambique. As anyone who has traveled knows, the people at the posts make you feel like you have ruined their day by coming to their country! Here we were with such enthusiasm. We thought the Africans would just welcome us with big arms and be so happy we had left America to come to their country, but that was not the case. We had to spend so much time filling out paperwork and going through customs and waiting. There was a young teenager that was at the border begging. She was obviously an AIDS patient, and was so thin that she could hardly walk. Her legs and arms were like sticks. She was too weak to talk; the only sound she could make was to meow like a cat. You talk about culture shock- it was pretty hard to explain that one to a three and six-year-old - two kids that had just left America and had been on the continent for just a few days.

Arrival In Beira To Begin Language School

We did make it in to Mozambique, after eight hours on the road. The missionaries knew we would not be able to stay by ourselves yet, as we did not know how to drive on the wrong side of the road, and we didn't know how to filter our water and all those things. They let us stay with them for five nights and they taught us many things. I will never forget calling my parents from their phone to tell them we had arrived in Mozambique and were safe. The connection was so bad and all I could hear was their tiny little voices. They seemed a million miles away, and they were. I tried to be strong and positive, but my heart was breaking inside. All I could think about was that I would not be home for three or four more years. I cried myself to sleep many nights. But it was a blessing to be in the Hooten household for those days. They had family devotions at night and the peace in their home really ministered to us. As we sat around in the family room during devotions, God reassured us that He would take care of us.

We tried to follow the advice of seeing people through God's eyes, as we were surrounded by people. In my first e-mails home, I wrote to my parents that I couldn't believe there were black people everywhere! What I meant was that, we lived in an apartment on the second floor, and the family on the first floor had many people in their apartment. The mother of the family and some of her friends or family would take a nap outside in our driveway, lying on grass mats. It was cooler outside with the breeze, than to rest in the hot concrete house. The family had two grown sons that were unemployed, and they would hang out on the outside steps leading up to our apartment. Behind every house was servant's quarters. The families in the apartments would own these quarters, but would rent them out to other families to gain a small income. So in these tiny concrete rooms in the back of our apartments were more families. They all did their washing on the roof of the servant's quarters and the clotheslines were up there. So when they were washing their clothes on the roof, they were on the same level as us on the second floor. So they would stare at us from the roof! They all cooked with fires outside, so you always smelled the smoke and the wind would blow the ashes around. The family below us had many visitors everyday. We wondered what they were stopping by to do, or buy. We found out that they were making homemade beer below us, and the mother of the house had a huge business selling the beer. It was quite upsetting to live in this situation and to know what was happening all around us. It was like you could never escape and have some quiet time!

We had night guards that watched our house while we slept just to be a presence and to deter thieves. Many times we would keep the front door open, to let some fresh air in, and he would be sitting just outside the screened door. Many nights we would talk to him, and we got to be quite close to Rodriquez. He taught us many of the Portuguese choruses, which was a huge help, since they are not written down. (Thus he was a great asset in helping us with the language.)

One of the first orders of business was learning how to drive in a foreign culture. Not only do you drive on the other side of the road, but the steering wheel is also on the other side of the car! Plus the car that we had was a manual shift, so you were shifting with the other hand. Plus there are all the foreign traffic signs, and all the different rules of the road.

Because of the people all around, Timothy and Grace were scared to go outside. And without a TV and a lot of toys, it made for long days. The children would refuse to go outside and would just follow me around the apartment. For those first few weeks, they were too scared to go down the hall, or even to their room. The main problem was that there were so many little boys outside and Timothy would want to play, but with the language barrier, he couldn't talk to them. Finally, after a few months, he got brave and went outside and played soccer with them. There were never any girls out. But one day we saw a little girl peering out of her house, so we ran outside to see if she would come play. Sidewalk chalk does wonders to break the ice, when you can't talk to the other child! It was such a relief when they began to play with the neighborhood children – we couldn't have gone on like we were with them refusing to go outside!

It was amazing though, to move across the ocean, and to have a furnished apartment and truck and everything we needed provided for us. The missionaries had prepared our house with everything we needed - even a water filter, mosquito nets, a phone, pots and pans- literally everything. They helped us set up a bank account and registered our children for school. For several months, since we could not speak the language, Bob would do our banking for us and pay our bills. They really were a huge help. When we first arrived, we were given an older truck to drive. After a few months, they saw that we needed another newer one. To get a truck with all the features that you needed to have in Mozambique, Bob, the Baptist business manager, had to drive down to Johannesburg,

South Africa. The truck had been shipped from Japan to the port in Durban, South Africa. Then it was sent up to Johannesburg, in the middle of the country. It was a two day drive for Bob to get to Johannesburg. It would take him ten days to get all the work done on it and then return. That is if everything went as planned! He had appointments each day to have something else done to it. He had to: tint the windows (for safety and heat issues), put a camper shell on it, put an extra fuel tank (since you can drive for hours, even days without seeing a gas station), get two extra rims and tires, put a winch on it (so that you can be pulled out of muddy or sandy holes), put a new extra heavy bumper on it (to be pulled out when stuck), and get the alarm system on it. Each thing was done at a different place and it was very time consuming to wait for all these things to be done. It was hard for us to realize that he would be away from his family for two weeks, just because he was doing us a favor. Before we got here, I never thought about that there had to be missionaries that do all these important "behind the scene" things.

We did eventually get settled and the children got settled into their schools. We had a nice apartment and met some beautiful people. The African church greeted us so warmly on Sunday mornings, and the English missionary fellowship that met on Sunday nights was such a treat. We lived less than a half of a mile from the beach and it was so beautiful to see it every day. Open sewage flowed into the beach in the town, so even though we couldn't swim in the beach, it was a beautiful sight! When passing it, we tried not to think about the sewage.

At times it was quite difficult to entertain the children. They did go to school until 1:00, but the afternoons and nights were long. I remember one time just going to the airport to see a plane land – now that is boredom! And the children kept asking for their grandparents. My parents had a trip planned, so I would tell them that Mi-mi and Pa-pa would be there soon. Finally one day Grace said, " Mi-mi and Pa-pa are taking such a long time to get here, maybe we should just go there instead." I was beginning to think that too. She prayed nightly for them to have a safe trip there.

All new missionaries that come to a country come with such a desire to immediately change the world and start work! It just didn't dawn on us that we would not be able to even speak to the people, so how could we do anything? Except for the other missionaries, no one spoke English. You are at a handicap when you can't even go to the market to buy things or figure out how to use their money. (Try figuring out how much things cost, when the exchange rate is 25,000 meticais to one dollar!) You can't speak to your neighbors or anyone! When everyone was speaking another language, we felt so lost and began to wonder if we would ever get the language. To communicate with our house worker, I would have to draw pictures on a piece of paper as to what I needed for her to do. The houseworker would go to the market for us, and she would buy the vegetables. She knew how to barter for them, and at that point, we couldn't even communicate what we wanted, so we sure couldn't have figured out how much they cost. Everything was in a foreign language- even how much things cost, and nothing was written down. So you couldn't just see a sign that said 75,000 meticais, and then begin counting it out. You had to ask the seller how much the things were, and then you had to know your Portuguese numbers well enough to catch what he said, and then give him the appropriate amount. So I would draw her the shopping list. I had crayons and would draw orange carrots, brown potatoes, green cabbage, and yellow bananas! It worked well until I could speak! You literally feel helpless, because as a grown adult, you couldn't mail a letter by yourself, buy groceries, or even talk to the maid and guard at your house. There were no street signs and no maps. The bakery was on one street, the vegetables at another and the meat at another. It took a while to figure out how to do the basic things of life.

We arrived in rainy season, and during this season, many water-borne diseases broke out due to the rising water levels. The water becomes contaminated and the people drink it and cook with it, as they have no alternative. Cholera often comes in epidemics, and is usually worse in older children and adults. Cholera broke out the first few months we were there. It was such a terrible epidemic, that hundreds, even thousands died. You can live after getting cholera, but must get treatment fast. Cholera tents were set up all over the city, since the one big hospital was full. Because the disease causes such terrible "rice water diarrhea", they usually are put in tents outside. But people did not get to the hospital quickly enough, and many died before getting help. The morgue was so full, that behind the hospital, they put several huge trash dumpsters - about 10 feet high and about 10 feet around. They began to throw the dead bodies in there, as they had nowhere else to put them. They were dying so fast, the families couldn't even identify the dead. I can't tell you how traumatic this was to see it and smell it - all the while not being able to tell Timothy and Grace what those big black dumpsters were for when they asked. I would write back home about the cholera, and I remember saying how many had died each day, and then one day, I got to write that it had subsided, and not as many were dying.

The best way to prevent cholera is to put bleach in the drinking water and make it clean. As missionaries, we put together little kits of bleach and other hygiene items and went door to door throughout the villages and gave them out and explained to the people how to prevent this terrible epidemic. It was a wonderful ministry to talk with the people and try to help them understand this epidemic. We prayed with the sick.

Beira used to be quite a tourist attraction before the civil war. Its beautiful white sand beaches, the restaurants and hotels were quite famous. But no one can underestimate what 25 years of war does to a country. The lack of medical care and poor roads with huge potholes are just two of the effects. The others are unclean water and weak electricity. We had to get used to the regular power outages, but thankfully had a gas stove, so we could at least cook. Our fear was that it would be off so long that our things in the freezer would ruin. The meat in there had to be bought from Zimbabwe - an 8-hour trip, so you did not want it to ruin!

The government at one point had been communist and this too affected the country tremendously. Many times the shopkeepers and others would not be friendly, or customer driven. You would feel like you were bothering them by coming into their shop.

On top of these difficulties, you also had to deal with the heat. We arrived in January at the height of the summer. We left America during its coldest time, so it took quite a while to adjust from 30 degrees to 100 degrees and even higher on some days. I think the thing that is so difficult about the heat is that it goes on for so many days and there is no respite. There is no such thing as central air. We did have a window unit air conditioner in our bedroom and in the living room area, but the one in the living room rarely worked.

So it was very nice to run the AC in our bedroom at night to sleep. We had to move the children's beds into our bedroom, because they couldn't sleep in that heat. With my sleeping children under their mosquito net, I loved to write e-mails at night. E-mails would connect me to home. During the day, the coolest place was to ride around in our car with the AC on, so we did that many days! But the heat can really make you irritable, as it is unbearable day after day. The worst part was the 100% humidity. After I cooked supper many nights, I was too wet with sweat to have the desire to even eat one bite. There was no AC at the children's schools and this affected Timothy's ability to focus and learn.

The poverty also was very difficult to bear. You began to feel guilty for having food on the table, nice clothes and a proper house. It really begins to play on your mind and you feel guilty when you know thousands around you are hungry. One day, right after arriving in Beira, we were walking around the vegetable market with our pastor. He was giving us a language lesson and helping us to know how to buy vegetables and what their normal price should be. Suddenly, three little boys under eight years of age, came up to me and grabbed my neck and ripped off my gold cross necklace! I was so grieved about this, as it had been a gift from my husband. They grabbed my neck so hard, that it was sore for days. I kept replaying that incident in my mind. I prayed for those little boys - who had probably been sent out to steal by their families. I wondered that night, if they sold it and had bought food, or possibly alcohol for their families. I was sick to my stomach. The Mozambican pastor kept apologizing and felt so terrible. But I knew in my heart, that I had left my home and parents, to tell little boys like those thieves about Jesus. Another time, while walking around the market, some little boys put their hands in Timothy's short pockets to try to see if they could get anything. There were little bands of these street children and they would mob you. Several times while we were shopping downtown, gangs of little boys surrounded our car and when we opened the door to get out, they reached their hands in the car. Another day they surrounded us when we drove up to park, and when we got out, they punched a button on the door which makes the door not close, and they tried to rob us.

Due to all the theft, one of the hardest things to get used to was all the keys that you had to carry around. You had to literally lock up everything. Just to get into our car and start it, you would first hit a switch to demobilize the alarm. Then we had four keys just to get in the car- one for the door, one for the ignition, one for the immobilizer and one for the gear lock. Then to get out of the garage, you had to unlock the padlock that kept the iron doors secure, and then you had to manually open them. Then to get gas, you had to unlock the fuel tank, because people would try to siphon your gas. Then after buying items, you had to lock them in the canopy on the way home- that was another key!

At our house, there were more keys. We had a key for the wooden outside doors, and then a key for the iron burglar bar gate. Then we would lock our bedrooms when we were away, so even if someone got in the house, they would not be able to steal the valuables in our bedroom. If we were going to be away for the day, we would lock the valuables in a bedroom, so the houseworker could not steal them. Then later, when we moved to our permanent home, each outside building had another key - the laundry room, the school room, and the two storerooms with Mike's agricultural tools, and our bikes. Then there was a key on the container that held all our Bibles and books for the churches. Then there was a key on the water cistern, so no one could steal our water. Then if we were going to ride our bikes into town, we had to have locks for them. We also had a lock on the outside gate. So it was very stressful to carry around all these keys.

One of the most evident sights of poverty is the Grande Hotel in Beira. It was three streets away from our house, and from our second floor apartment, we could see it in plain view. It is a huge hotel that was built in 1952, and was billed the "pride of Africa." It was widely regarded as the largest and most exquisite hotel on the continent. It was a popular destination for the wealthy Portuguese and British. Yet, nine years after its opening, the hotel was forced to close due to civil unrest associated with the Portuguese Colonial War. Approximately 3,000 took refuge in the hotel during the war, and have to this day resisted any attempt by the government to remove them.

To see pictures of how the hotel used to be, compared to how it is now, is shocking. There is of course no electricity at the hotel, so it is a weird sight to see it at night lit up with thousands of candles. According to foreign visitors that went to the hotel recently, virtually everything of any value has been looted from the hotel, including its marble and bathroom tiles, wooden flooring, sinks and bathtubs. The former pool now serves as a water collector for clothes washing, and the former pool bar as a urinal. The hotel has experienced structural damage, and trees grow out of the terraces and floors have collapsed. Goats wander in and out of the lobby by the once marble stairway. The visitors said that the floor was covered in about 6 inches of open sewage. They say the smell in the hotel is unbearable, as thousands of people live with no sewer system or running water. We would hear and see this place, and it was really unnerving to be so close to such an atrocity. There was a pet monkey on a string that kept us entertained as he ran around on one of the verandas.

I had never lived without medical care readily available, and this is a blessing most people don't fully appreciate until you don't have it. In a developed country, it is such a comfort to know that if you break a leg, or need an emergency operation to save your life, you know you can get it. But when you have two small kids in a country rife with malaria and other diseases, you honestly begin to worry. The first person in our family to get malaria was Timothy. Fortunately in Beira, we had a Baptist nurse named Nancy Carley. She was so good to our family. When Timothy got sick, she came over to our house and pricked Timothy's finger to get a blood sample. Then she and I drove about an hour one way to a missionary clinic. It was quite a mission to get to that clinic with the pot holes and detours that at times made the journey impossible. By her coming to the house to get the blood sample, the sick person could then stay home in bed, while she and I drove that awful drive to the mission clinic to get the results. She gave us so much advice on which medicines to take, and was always available - even in the middle of the night. God put a Baptist missionary nurse on our street that first year, and I can't thank Him enough. The health concerns were great, but at least we knew that with our mission board, there was an excellent air evacuation policy – they would be committed to getting us to whatever medical care we needed in the event of an emergency.

It was very painful for us all when Timothy came down with malaria. We were at a big meeting, and people from the mission board in Virginia had come out to meet with us. It was a very important meeting and they had gotten some young missionaries (Journeyman) to care for all the MK's while we were in all-day meetings. On this particular day, they had taken all the MK's to the pool. It was a very hot day, and this was the best way to entertain all the kids. When we went to the pool at 5:00 p.m. to pick up the kids after the meeting, we found Timothy lying on the side of the pool in the direct sun. All the other kids were swimming and playing and the Journeyman were playing with the other kids. He was burning up with fever; later we took it and it was 104. Then he began to shiver and shake. We asked the Journeyman why they did not call us or why they hadn't tried to care for him by helping him to lay in the shade. We were furious! He was so sick, and they had completely ignored him. He did vomit a lot and needed a shot, but we didn't have one. Nancy drove all over town trying to find a pharmacist that had the shot she needed for him. Timothy did recover after he got the right medicine. But dealing for the first time with my child having malaria, was very traumatic. That night I cried myself to sleep as I felt like a terrible mother to bring my little children over here, subjecting them to these diseases. I remembered those horrible words that man had said to me in North Carolina, that my parents had raised a fool. I felt like Jacob that night, wrestling with God.

The nurse, Nancy Carley, gave us very good advice that we have never forgotten. She told us that God knew where we were - in a poor, war-torn country with very little medical care. She reminded us that God knows the needs of our family and the ages of our children. She said she has never known a missionary or a missionary child in our organization to die for lack of medical care. She said that God, because he knew where we were, would take care of us. I held onto those words and they became such a comfort to me, and sustained us through many medical emergencies!

Grace had two mishaps that first year. The first time, she had a hairline fracture in her collarbone after a fall playing leapfrog with Timothy. A Mozambican doctor came to the house on his red motorcycle to examine her. In the initial examination, he wanted to check her general reflexes - hitting below the knee. He didn't have any medical tools, so he asked us for a fork. We got him one and he hit her knee with the fork- and this obviously does the same thing as a doctor's hammer. But to a 3-year-old in great pain, she thought this doctor was going to stick her with a fork!

Another time she cut open her foot by stepping on a metal toy. She needed stitches to close the wound. On that particular day, we could find no doctor. Nancy tried and tried to help us find someone to stitch her foot up. Finally, another international who had some medical training came over. I had the stitches and needles that I had brought with me for days like this. We put a sheet on the dining room table and turned it into an operating table. All of the adults held her down while she screamed in pain. Without any anesthesia, the lady began to try to sew up Grace's foot. She tried many different needles that I had, but after an hour or so, she didn't have a needle big enough to go through the toughness of a foot - they kept bending or breaking. So when the last needle broke, we realized there was nothing we could do. We put those butterfly bandages on it and wrapped it tightly and prayed hard!

The other effects of not having medical care were that others did not have it as well when they needed it. It was normal to see disfigured people begging. Sometimes the disfigurement would be shocking, especially to Timothy and Grace. There was one man that roamed around Beira that had been severely burned on the face. He would use his shocking appearance to spur people on to giving him money. He only had one eye due to the fire and one side of his face was so stretched that it hung down to near his shoulders. We did hear that one of the organizations in town raised money to fly him to Europe because a plastic surgeon had been found that would operate on him for free. We did see him after his surgery, and it was so much better.

Another tragedy happened while we were out of the country getting supplies, our freezer went out. During a power outage, one of the breakers or fuses had blown and the freezer went out. It was full of meat. Since we had to buy the meat in Zimbabwe, one tended to stock up, since that was an eight-hour round trip to the butcher! Mike happened to be away at that time when I arrived home with the children. I opened the front door, and the smell was unbelievable. It immediately made me sick. I was too afraid to go in the house to investigate. I didn't know if someone had died in the house or if it was an animal or what. I was terrified! Luckily the phone was near the front door, so I just stood by the door and called the other missionaries for help. Unfortunately, one missionary was down in his back and couldn't come help, and no one else was home. So I had to be brave and walk down the long corridor of our house to investigate. I am terrified of mice and was so afraid of what I would find. But as I turned the corner to walk down the hall, I saw all this blood and water on the floor, and so many maggots. I realized the freezer had gone out and all that meat had ruined. The smell of all that rotten meat stayed in the house from that day until the day we moved six months later. We tried everything to get rid of the smell. It did get better, but you could still smell it. I did find a maid to come clean it up and she was so helpful, but I had to pay her big bucks! What do people do without the Lord Jesus? He literally carried us during this time. It may sound like a small thing, but it was quite a traumatic thing for me to handle alone with Timothy and Grace!

The reason that Mike was not with me at the time is of importance to understand the situation where we lived. We had gone to Zimbabwe to shop for food and supplies. Theft was always a problem wherever we went. We had been staying in a guest house and to keep our laptop from being stolen, we hid it under the mattress. E-mail was my lifeline home and it was not going to be stolen over my dead body! But when we got ready to leave Zimbabwe and come back home to Mozambique, we accidentally left the computer under the guest house mattress. We were traveling with another missionary family, and they decided for Mike and the other man to go back to Zimbabwe to get the laptop, while the kids and I continued on towards home. He had to travel four hours back to the guest house, never knowing if it would still be there, or if the maids had found it and stolen it. Praise God, it was there. But this is why Mike wasn't with me, in those first few months when we were struggling to adjust.

It seemed we often had to drive into Zimbabwe for one thing or another. We had to go there to the US Embassy several times to get the necessary visa to live in Mozambique. The closest Embassy was eight hours away. One time we drove all that way to get our visas extended. To get our visa, the President of the Mozambique Baptist Convention had to write a letter saying that we had permission to be in the country. He wrote the letter, but forgot to get it stamped by the local proper official, and they would not accept it! We also went to Zimbabwe to get groceries, meat and milk. We couldn't get apples in Mozambique at the time, and I remember being so happy to drive to Zimbabwe and get apples for the children. We also had our post office box there, because it was safer for us to get our mail and packages there. If things would have been mailed to Mozambique, they were more than likely to get stolen. Our families would tell us that they mailed us a package long ago, and months later when we were in Zimbabwe we would go to the post office to collect them. One time we drove to Zimbabwe, just sure that we would get three packages that had been sent long ago, and when we got there, nothing had arrived yet. We were all about in tears to have received no mail or packages after driving for eight hours! During the cholera epidemic, we were afraid they would close the borders, to prevent the spread of disease. We were always scared of this, because Zimbabwe held so many things for us.

The reason we were in Beira was to study Portuguese. Our language teacher was a lady named Raquel - a missionary from Portugal. She lived in a very poor part of town, in some rundown apartments. I will never forget stepping over the sewage in the streets to get to her house. Language school is such a painful time! You feel you will never get it. She suffered from malaria a lot, and so did her little girl. One time, her daughter almost died. So we missed lots of lessons when either they were sick, or we were sick. One of the main components to learning another language is consistency. It was very hard to learn a language with so much sickness. Most people in Beira go to Zimbabwe a lot to get groceries or go to the doctor. So we missed classes often when either of us had to travel. But in her own way, she really tried to help us. Several times we ate lovely Portuguese lunches after our lessons. She introduced us to the wonderful Portuguese food. She really sacrificed to feed us shrimp and even one time, lobster. I so wanted to be able to cook like this - everything in coconut milk. But she wrote the recipes in Portuguese, so it was a while before I could understand how to make them! She tried to make the best of her situation in that apartment on the second floor. She had a big porch on the front of her house, and she kept a dog there and other little animals for her children, and lots of plants. She definitely was given lemons, and made lemonade out of her situation!

We studied the language with two other couples that were on their way to Angola- another country that was colonized by Portugal, thus speaking Portuguese. It means so much to have people go through this terrible time with you! One couple in particular was there with us most of the time, while the other couple moved on more quickly. The couple that was with us was Janice and Eddie Ray. They were experienced missionaries, and were transferring to Angola after being in another country. They fed us many a meal - I don't know how she did it - to make southern home cooking in the middle of Mozambique with such limited groceries! We are deeply indebted to them for their encouragement and love.

We went to Raquel every morning, and then at other times, had a conversant, that was just to talk with us. He was the local pastor of the First Baptist Church of Beira. He was an elderly, godly man. He found out how much I loved music, so each class, we would take out our Portuguese Baptist hymnals, and sing. It helped so much and it was a way I could really learn. It was so cool to sing all my favorite songs in another language - "What a Friend we have in Jesus", and others. We sang at every class, and to this day, I know the words of the great hymns in Portuguese. One Sunday, he wanted us to sing in church as a trio- he and Mike and I. We sang "To God be the Glory" in Portuguese in beautiful three-part harmony acapella. We did this after only three months of language. I remember writing to my mother in my e-mail that I hope the people know what in the heck we are singing about!

He would give us assignments to prepare for the next class. One night I got my night guard to help me with a devotional I was supposed to give in front of him the next day. I didn't want it to be full of errors, so I got the guard's help. The next day, he was quite impressed, but I had felt like I had cheated. But the most precious thing about him was that he would pray for us before we left our time together. He would pray for our children by name, and in the 12 months that we met with him, he never once failed to pray for Timóteo and Graça. This really ministered to us and we will never forget it.

From time to time, we would have tests in the language to see how we were doing. One time, we went out to eat with our language teacher and her husband to a restaurant. While there, we could only speak Portuguese. We had to greet the waiter and order everything in the language. During the meal, we could only converse in the language. Then after we ate, we had to ask for the bill and pay the correct amount of money. Talk about pressure! At other times during the year, we had to pass off a visit to the post office, bank, market, and hardware store. We had to greet the person in each store and ask for what we needed, pay the correct money, then saying the appropriate closings. Mike and I had to go in separately so as not to help each other!

As I have mentioned, the first time someone stole from us, was when the little boys ripped off my necklace in the market. But the second robbery was very traumatic. During our time in Beira, we had a wonderful houseworker. Houseworkers were essential, as there was so much that needed to be done- filtering water, buying vegetables in the open market, soaking and bleaching all the vegetables, washing all the dishes, and ironing all the clothes. (All clothes have to be ironed, because when they dry on the line, mango flies can lay eggs on your clothes. The clothes are then worn, and the eggs penetrate your skin, and turn into a worm that has to be removed!) So everything has to be ironed, even underwear! So a house worker is not just a luxury, but a necessity.

We had a wonderful lady named Ruth who worked for us. She was a lovely Christian, who really seemed to love the Lord. She went to church faithfully, and even had clothes that were printed, "I love Jesus", etc. She had material that she made a dress with that had pictures of Jesus on the cross. She was so good to us and came highly recommended. For the first eight months or so, things were going perfect. At times, she would keep the children while we were in class. One day we got home and Grace had painted Ruth's fingernails, each with a different color – using gold, green, and blue. She thought this was most strange, and we could tell she was having a hard time understanding these crazy Americans. She did really love Grace and Grace loved to try to talk to her and draw her pictures, which we saw as we visited her house one day, stuck up in her little straw roof.

She had one handicapped son, and we took him on as a project. We bought easy books for him, and many other things so that maybe he could learn to read. We bought both of them clothes and gave them things for their house. One time her roof was leaking and we went to her house and helped her fix it, as well as give her a little stove to cook on. We loved her so much, and she was so good to us. I would tell people in America about her and all she had done for us. Friends of mine and family would mail her things from America - like dresses and necklaces, etc. She didn't realize how good we treated her.

One day, she told me that her long lost husband had come back home from South Africa. He had gone down there to get work, and she hadn't heard from him in over 10 years. He was back and had found work and wanted her to join him in South Africa. She asked us to help her get a passport so she could go with him. We hated to lose her, but hoped she would have a better life in South Africa. One day we went to language school, and then came home as usual. When we got home, she seemed in a hurry to leave, so quickly said goodbye. Later that night, I went to turn on the radio, and realized it was gone. Then we began to search, and found so many things missing- our camera, video camera, Mike's electric razor, many canned goods, kitchen items, tape player, etc. When we added it all up, she had stolen over $3,000.00 worth of stuff. There are no words to describe the pain of this betrayal. It would have been better for a complete stranger to come in and steal from us, but this was a lady that had become a part of our family, and we had been so good to her. Needless to say, it took us a long time to get over this one.

I must say this was a very difficult time. This robbery was on top of the other difficulties and the pain of being away from our families. One day I was having a particularly difficult time. Our dear friends in language school with us, the Rays, kept trying to encourage us. They fed us and prayed for us, babysat for us, and visited us. One day, I was pouring out my heart to her about how I just wasn't going to make it. We had been through robberies, malaria, the freezer going out, Grace's two accidents, etc. This was on top of trying to learn a language, and feeling so stupid when you couldn't get it right. Janice Ray told me that in times like this, one must go back to the call of God, and remember that He has called you and He will therefore sustain you. I looked at her with all seriousness, and I told her that I was mad at the God that called me. I didn't even want to cling to my call, because at that point, I was mad at God for calling me to missions. She told me at that point, all she knew to do was pray for me. I got over this stage of culture shock and pain, and I am sure she is surprised today that we have been on the field for 11 years! Thank you Janice!

While Beira was a hard place to live, due to how rundown it was, there were bright spots. The food there is some of the best I have ever had in the world. It had a completely different taste than America food, and I grew to love it. (I also grew too!) I was sure I would lose weight in Africa, but that did not happen! The Portuguese people really know how to make pastries and little cakes and even after the war, some of these bakeries opened back up. Each Sunday after church, all the missionaries would go to lunch, and our goal was to try out every restaurant in town! The service was slow, because they wanted you to stay and eat several courses and just relax. They also had a pool there and we became members of the pool and enjoyed swimming there. It was right on the beach and also had a great restaurant. I would always feel so guilty swimming in such a beautiful pool, while the masses outside the gate were so poor.

Another blessing was that they actually had a hair salon in the train station! I had brought all my perm solutions and rollers with me and I went to this lady and tried to get her to understand that I needed a perm and she could use these perm kits. Since she would have never seen an American perm kit, I had gotten my language helper to write out explicit instructions on how to give me a perm. They usually turned out okay, but when she would ask me questions in Portuguese about what this instruction meant, I would just smile, because I didn't know how to answer back yet in Portuguese. I would sit there and just wonder what in the world my hair was going to look like, since she had no idea what she was doing, and she didn't understand my language teacher's writing! But believe it or not, my hair was never ruined or burned and by God's grace it looked okay.

Another funny thing was the amount of weird stuff you could find that had been imported into that city if you just looked. If you just walked the streets of these old, run down, unpainted shops, it was amazing what you could find. I have this gray patch in my hair that I have had since high school. To keep from having to dye the whole lot, I have always used colored mousse that you can just put on that one spot to help it blend in with the rest. One day, I had run out of the mousse I had brought with me. That day, we were walking around the city practicing our Portuguese. We went from store to store to see what they had. It would just be an Indian man or woman behind a counter with a few items. I looked back there, and this Indian man had bottles and bottles of the exact brown mousse that I use. God must have a sense of humor as he even cared for this smallest of needs. Yet, to me, it was a huge blessing to at least feel good about how I looked - even though I was far from home and still in culture shock.

There were many missionaries and other internationals in Mozambique. On Sunday nights, they had an English fellowship that met. We would sing praise choruses, and then the different missionaries would take turn preaching. Sometimes there would be 50-75 people there. They also had a Sunday School for the children. After being immersed in Portuguese all week long, it was such a blessing to sing in my heart language and have a sermon in English. We did many social events with this group, even celebrating the Fourth of July. We did a Christmas play and then went to the local orphanage and acted the story of Christmas out- complete with costumes. All of this was so good for Timothy and Grace. We even got together several times and played a big game of baseball – on a soccer field!

We met the nicest and most interesting people in this fellowship. One was a family named the Batis. He was Fijian and she was Canadian, and their children were the same ages as ours. We arrived in Beira in January, and they were out of the country then. But they returned the first of February and heard about this new family called the Boones. Someone happened to mention to her that Grace and I had birthdays in February, and how sad it must be that we had just arrived and were spending our birthdays when we still weren't sure about this Beira place! She arrived at our house on my birthday, February 11, with the most beautiful homemade cake. We had never met her before. That was the start of a very dear friendship that continues to this day.

Another person that was there was John Wickes, from America. He worked with the street children in Beira and lived with them in a shelter. He had been in Africa for many years. A few years before this, he had finally met and married a lady that had also come over to work with the street children. They were on their honeymoon in an animal park in Zimbabwe, when a buffalo came out of nowhere and goarded her and she died on their honeymoon. A book was written about her life. But he recovered from that, and was faithfully working with those boys. We would go as a family to the shelter and try to get to know the boys and we kind of adopted two of them that we would bring to our house to play. The last word we heard was that John was still in Mozambique, unmarried, helping these forgotten children.

Other missionaries and aid workers were there from many different countries and they worked with an organization called Food for the Hungry. Their international headquarters were in Beira and I find it no coincidence that Mike was able to meet these people and learn from them, since he was about to move to Mocuba to be an agricultural missionary. Everyone God brought in to our lives was for a purpose.

A special blessing that happened during that year was that I got to lead music at the English fellowship. They had a lady leading the music, but she and her family returned to England after some time. They asked me to choose the songs, play the keyboard, and lead the worship time. They sang mostly choruses, and it was such a blessing to get to know new songs from England and Australia and other places - since the fellowship was made up of people from all over the world. After being a Minister of Music in the states, I felt I would have to give that up to serve God- knowing that the African style of worship would be very different. But God gave this privilege back to me to lead worship- there I was in Beira, Mozambique in a country that only speaks Portuguese, and I was getting to lead worship in English for 75 other internationals that were also blessed to hear music in their language. God was so amazing to give me this privilege!

The schools in Beira were wonderful. When you drive through the city, and see the unpainted buildings, many of them crumbling, and the filth, you just wouldn't believe that there were enough internationals or Mozambicans that could support these schools.

Grace went to a Portuguese preschool. She had a little uniform and immediately began to speak Portuguese. At age four, she knew it before any of us. If she wanted to play with friends, she was going to have to learn their language. We couldn't talk to her teachers for a long time, and when we would pick her up, we would just smile, and they would smile back! She had the nicest workbooks from Portugal, and she really learned a lot.

One day, we went to pick her up from school, and she was hot with a fever. I was so upset that the school hadn't called us to come pick her up - not that we had cell phones or anything, but still they could have maybe tracked us down. When I asked her why she didn't tell her teacher that she was sick, and to please call her mom, she told me that she didn't know how to say all that in Portuguese! I felt so bad! So I wrote a little note and stuck it in her bag that she carried every day. It said- "I am sick. Please call my mother". *Eu estou doente, por favor liga a minha mãe!* All she had to do was show them this note in Portuguese next time she was sick! We couldn't communicate with the principal or the teachers very much, but you could tell they really loved Grace. They did a secular Christmas play in December, and all the children were little bees - go figure this for Christmas. But anyway, the principal proudly told me that they had picked Grace to be the queen bee - she had a special costume, different from the others! I don't know what bees have to do with Christmas; we knew we were in a foreign country.

Timothy also had a phenomenal school, the Beira International Primary School- BIPS. The teacher was an American. She lived right on the beach in a lovely two-story house, with a huge yard - maybe an acre. It was fenced in, and her yard was a child's paradise. It was landscaped like a botanical garden, but still had room for the children to play. She had five old Mozambican dug-out canoes in the yard that she had planted flowers in. Many days, they met outside and made things, and then climbed trees or went to the beach to watch the fishermen come in for the day with their catch. They would hike to the lovely lighthouse and then come back and write a story about the lighthouse. It was hands-on learning. There were only about ten children in the school, and they were from all over the world. They put on the most wonderful programs. One day they did a program on water. They had dug out a small pond and they had each made homemade boats for the pond. They made a tall lighthouse out of cardboard and painted it to match the real Beira lighthouse across the street – they even put a real light in the top, like the original one. After the program, we had a lunch, and her husband provided fresh crabs for us all. The amazing thing was that she was only in Beira for three years- the school opened the year before we got there, and then we were there the second and part of the third year, and then she left! I am convinced God put her there at that perfect time for Timothy. He was a very active six- year-old, and with all the outdoor activities, that was how he learned. She had a wonderful library and art supplies and had all the traditional African instruments for music - what a lady. She hated to see us move at the end of our time in Beira. She told Timothy that she enjoyed him so much; that he was the reason she had a good day each day. I will never be able to forget how much God provided for my children in the midst of a very difficult situation in Beira.

It was a blessing to begin to be used of God even while in language school. As is the case in many churches worldwide, the church in Beira was short a few Sunday School teachers. A few months after we arrived, before we could really speak Portuguese well, we were expected to help with the Sunday School. What would happen is that the teacher wouldn't show up, and they would turn to Mike and I, since we were missionaries, and expect us to teach! I can remember getting someone to read the passage, and then we would just read the lesson verbatim out of the book. Then I would say a very few sentences, and then dismiss them – I had said all I could say! The first Sunday we got out in 20 minutes – just 40 minutes early. On Saturdays, at the Women's meeting, I was expected as well to take my turn, but then again, we were fortunate to have books, and I could prepare ahead of time.

The pastor of the Baptist church, who was our language helper, was such a dear man. His daughter got engaged while we were there. Because of this, he wanted me to do some teaching on Christian marriage, and to include the subject of abstinence before marriage. Many people would not want this subject talked about in church, but he clearly came to me and asked me to do a series on Tuesday nights during the Bible study to speak on purity. I can remember working very hard with my language teacher, to say everything correctly. He must have thought I did a good job, because soon after that, he asked me to do a series on world missions. He wanted the people to see a world map and know which countries are open to missionaries and which are closed. He wanted me to share some of the needs around the world. We prayed for the unreached people groups, and it was a wonderful time. I also spoke during the Christmas service on the different names of Christ. All of this was so wonderful to be given the chance to use and try out my language skills. People many times don't give you an opportunity until you are completely fluent, but you can't become fluent, unless you are given an opportunity to speak! It is a vicious cycle, but I was fortunate to be given the opportunity to break into it!

Our church was in the middle of building a new building and it was a blessing to be involved in that. They sure did need a new building; the other one was built up off the ground and the old wooden floors had huge holes in them that people fell through. It was really dangerous. Mike also preached at one of the little missions outside of town, and did a baptism for them, since they didn't have a pastor. We were so grateful to be given opportunities to be used of God even during language school. We are grateful to all those dear people that were patient with us when we butchered their precious language! It was a blessing to be involved with the church in various outreach efforts. One day, the church set up a volleyball net on the beach and played a pick-up game with people passing by. After the game, they passed out tracts and tried to witness to those that had played.

We also loved having the Mozambicans over to show them the *JESUS* film. None of them had seen the film. To visually see the stories of Jesus, and to see his death and resurrection for the first time was such a blessing. And to hear it in their own language-Jesus and all the characters speaking Portuguese! They would say, "I did not know Jesus spoke Portuguese". I said, "He invented Portuguese!"

It was a blessing to be a part of the First Baptist Church of Beira. We got close to a couple in the church. She was expecting a baby and when we heard she had gone to the hospital to deliver, we went to visit her. When we got there, she had already delivered and they told her she had twins. But she was so distraught, because they told her that one of them was born dead, while the other was born healthy. In the commotion of the birth, they had whisked the "dead" baby away, and she never even saw it. She was so troubled about this, because she just wanted to see the other baby. Later, as she inquired about it, one of the nurses told her that the baby didn't die, but that it was sick and had problems, and that it was taken away to another ward in the hospital. The pastor and I went from floor to floor of the big Beira hospital, asking everyone we could find to tell us where the baby was. Finally, another nurse told us that the baby was dead, and that it had been taken to the morgue. The pastor and I went to the city morgue to see if the body was there, and they said that no baby had died in the past week and that no baby had been brought there. We went back to the hospital to try to comfort the mother. She was just beside herself that one of her babies had been taken away. We finally went to the administration and told them that we must know what happened to the baby- that we had searched the hospital and the morgue. She finally told us that they felt that twins were a curse, and that they knew that the mother could not sufficiently nurse two babies, due to malnutrition. So they had taken the baby and not fed it and just allowed it to die naturally. This was such a culture shock and such an atrocity that really grieved me.

Mike's Accident

While the children and I waited in Beira and I continued on with language school, Mike flew on up to Mocuba and started working on our house. It was in quite bad shape and he wanted to get the water and electricity working before we got there. He was driving back and forth to the city of Quelimane (key-luh-MAH-knee), where our missionary friends, the Dinas lived, to get supplies and take showers, etc. It was a two-hour drive to Quelimane where the hardware store was. One night, at about dusk, he was returning back to Quelimane from Mocuba and was pulling a trailer. One of the most difficult things about Mozambique is the driving. There are so many people in the roads, even young children unsupervised. There are animals and pot holes and people everywhere. It is not uncommon to hear of drivers hitting people that are in the road. I know of four other missionaries that did - with some of the people even dying. As Mike was driving, a little boy wanted to cross the road. He stopped when he saw Mike's truck, but the little boy didn't see the trailer behind the truck. He ran right into the trailer and was knocked to the ground. Mike heard the loud thud. Mike stopped the car and just knew he was dead. Mike could not speak too much Portuguese, and there were no cell phones to call for help. He scooped up the child, and rushed him to the hospital. Then the police got involved and wanted to prosecute Mike. They impounded the car and made Mike spend the night in the prison courtyard. Luckily, John Dina came to the rescue, to talk to the police and he even spent the night in the prison with Mike. Mike saw many rats scurrying around.

Another part of this story is that Mike had flown up, and didn't have his driver's license with him. Because there is so much theft, you don't carry extra documents like that if you are not going to need them. He just briefly drove that one time, not even remembering he had taken his license out of his wallet. So the police charged him for driving without a license. To get him out of prison, I had to fax a copy of his driver's license up there, and that sufficed.

I only got the call late at night while I was alone with the children in Beira - 14 hours away. I called Nancy, the missionary nurse who lived on our street, and she immediately came over. She prayed with me and we entrusted Mike into God's hands, as we did not know if the boy would live or die, or what would happen to Mike. Of course, I didn't sleep a wink all that night. Missionary Bob Evans quickly began to help also - to get a copy of the license and to fax it to the necessary officials in Quelimane. I am indebted to them for their help.

Immediately when I got the news, I opened the wooden door and told our night guard about what happened. He showed such concern. Crying in public, in their culture, is just not done, and they don't know how to handle it when an international cries. As I wept and wept, he just calmly kept talking and telling me God was in control, and he prayed for me and for the situation. God greatly used him that night. All night long I heard him singing praise songs to God right outside our front door and it was such a comfort.

The little boy ended up being okay. Mike paid the hospital bills, and checked on him after he was discharged from the hospital. The policeman that worked on Mike's case was the son of a pastor.

He was sympathetic to Mike and he was therefore able to leave the prison the next morning. (Mike saw this policeman again a few years later, and he wanted a Bible and Mike gave him one, and thanked him again for his role in the saga.) Mike was due to fly back to Beira in a few days, but we were concerned he would not be able to leave Quelimane, since the case was still pending. But they allowed John Dina to stand in for Mike and quickly the case was over after the bills were paid. We know that God put a Christian policeman on this case, as at times these things can turn very ugly, as the family tries to abuse the system and demand a great deal of money. But the witnesses clearly said that Mike was not negligent - that when he saw the boy, he slowed down, and that is was completely the boy's fault. But even in these cases, the police can side with the family and great harm can be done to the driver. So we praise God for this angel in a police uniform.

I will never forget the night we went to the airport to pick up Mike from this trip to Quelimane and Mocuba. I couldn't wait to see him, to see how he was after such a traumatic event. As we got to the airport, the electricity went off due to a major thunderstorm - the whole airport was pitch black, even the runway lights didn't work. We didn't know how the plane was going to land with no lights. Mike was flying in an old plane and the lights on the plane didn't work either. (This had been a hard trip for Mike as he was on a very old plane. Mike said that the door of the plane wouldn't even close- he could see the ground through the crack in the door!) So as I stood in the pitch-black airport, trying to comfort a four and six-year-old, this plane just descended from the sky and landed safely. God is a great God to protect us through all these things!

Needless to say, Mike was traumatized after hitting this child. It was hard for him to drive, because he kept remembering that thump when the child hit his truck. It took great prayer to help Mike work through this experience. It is always beneficial to look at the good things that happened during a tragedy, and one of those was the kindness of the Dinas. Who would spend the night with you in a dirty Mozambican prison? Now that is a true friend.

Chapter 6

MOVING TO MOCUBA

AFTER WE "graduated" from language school, we were able to move to Mocuba - the city where we felt so called to. We flew in a small missionary plane, a 6-seater, to our new home. We had gotten a little dog, and named him Beira, so we would always remember the year we spent there. We had to go through so much red tape to transport this dog to Mocuba, and it almost didn't happen. I think my kids would have been crushed had that have happened! (Unfortunately, after all that, the little dog was stolen from our house in the first month we were in Mocuba!) The pilot of course was flying the plane, but at one point, he told Timothy to lean over and grab the steering wheel and "drive the plane". That was pretty cool for a seven-year-old!

Mocuba is a small town of about 20,000 people, although it is very hard to do an official census. It had one main street that went through town and on this street was about 50 nice cement houses with tin roofs. In the days of colonialism, the Portuguese lived in these. Mocuba is built on a beautiful river and there is big bridge on the outskirts of the city leading to Mocuba. On this main street, there is a downtown section. There is a round-about that has a fountain in the middle. Around this round-about, was the police station, the beautiful Catholic cathedral, and the town hall. The town hall was a nice building with a huge outdoor staircase leading up to the second floor. On both sides of the staircase was a pair of elephant tusks. They are huge, and would be worth so much money because ivory is very valuable! We heard that the last administrator (mayor) , in the middle of the night, stole the ivory and fled the town! I would think it would be pretty hard to sneak out of town with ivory tusks that are 7 feet tall! He was found with them and they were returned, and he was fined and put in prison. They say Mocuba was a pretty town before the war, but now most of the buildings are not painted and many of the shops are empty.

We found an old Portuguese house to fix up. The church had been very involved in trying to help us find adequate housing. Since the church had requested a missionary, they assumed they would have to build us a house. When we first went up to Mocuba to look for housing, they told us they would build us a house. But we said they didn't have to do that!

The house we decided to rent had belonged to a Portuguese policeman. As I walked in, I recalled how all the Portuguese had to flee during the war, and walk away from everything they owned. I walked in to that huge house and was actually sad, thinking about how a family somewhere had been forced out of this house, and how they had lost all their furniture and everything in it. After the Portuguese fled Mozambique, the Mozambican people just moved into these houses. It is called "squatter's rights". The present owner was a Mozambican man that had worked for the police force, and knew the house, and the minute the Portuguese family fled, he moved in with his family. So we had to pay the equivalent of $400.00 a month to this Mozambican family that now "owned" the house. It all seemed quite unfair to me!

There is no way to describe what shape this house was in when we went in to see if we wanted to rent it. There was a motorcycle in the house. The outside of the house had not been painted in probably 20 years, and it was so ugly. They had cooked on an open fire inside the house, so it had blackened walls from the smoke. On the floor, on big tarps, they were drying their corn meal, and it was covered in bugs and cockroaches. The plumbing didn't work, so there was no running water to the house. The bathtub was black. The only light they had was one bulb that hung from a string in the middle of each room. Many of the windows were broken. The kitchen was outside, and it just had a cement counter and then a huge chimney so you could cook with wood. So there was no kitchen in the house, and no cabinets, etc. Outside, in the yard, there was no grass or flowers, just dirt. Next to the house was an open field. Mike was excited about using this for his demonstration farm. But since there was no trash pick up, we noticed that this extra field was the trash heap. It had all been buried, to look nice, but an inch below the surface, were cans and bottles and cardboard, etc. We even found a hood and windshield of an entire car. The windshield was broken and glass was everywhere. They had a few outside buildings to store things, but termites had overtaken them and the termite mounds were taller than me and covered half of the little rooms.

But I think we could have handled all this if we knew we would have e-mail capabilities so we could communicate with our family. When we went to apply for a phone for our house, we were told we were number 257 on the waiting list! And she said only a few become available a year, because they only become available when someone moves or dies! So obviously, this was worst than all the other difficult things. We would have to take our laptop to Quelimane, which was 2 hours away, and down load our messages when we got there. It ended up being about once a month, sometimes twice.

We rented the house, because we knew with a coat of paint, and with lots of work, it would be a nice house. It was structurally sound and in a good location. It was a split-level house with very high ceilings and this was nice to help with the ventilation. Also, under the house were two separate rooms and bathroom. We knew this would be great for us to use in home schooling, and also for a guest room. So we saw the potential.

As I've written, Mike went up a month early to begin to fix this house up before we arrived. He drove our truck up there, pulling a trailer full of our possessions. Right before we were to move to our permanent location, we received many lovely boxes of food items from Ephesus Baptist Church. As we were packing them in the trailer, the nationals saw all the food, and they asked us if where we were going had no food! This food was such a lifesaver for us!

While Mike repaired our rental house, he camped inside in a sleeping bag, and a worker cooked him rice and gravy for every meal. He had no refrigerator or any other comforts. He had an electrician rewiring the house and putting light fixtures in. He had a man to fix the broken windows, and then to install burglar bars.

He had another man painting the inside of the house. He had a man outside building wooden cabinets for us to make a kitchen inside. This same carpenter was building school desks for the children, and a frame for our waterbed mattress. He had another crew building a cistern to store water and another plumber to replumb the house so that you could use the toilets and bathtub. He was the supervisor and contractor of all of this, as he was the one that would buy the supplies. If you gave them money to go buy a bag of cement, they were never able to bring you a receipt and the correct change! Mike learned this the hard way! He gave one worker some money to go get some things for him, and he didn't have any change, so he asked him to bring the change back. He came back with no change, saying he ran into a family member, and in their culture, he had to help his family with the rest of the money! So Mike knew if we were going to have any money left after this venture, he would have to oversee it all!

Finally the time came for us to fly up to begin our lives in Mocuba. We had grown to love Beira and were actually sad to say goodbye to good friends. Oh how we would miss the pool, the restaurants, English fellowship, the kid's schools, and our phone and Internet connection! We would have none of this in Mocuba. We arrived with our little dog, Beira, and saw that actually, although Mike had worked like a Trojan for a month, it was still very bad. Things move very slowly in Mocuba, because you have to get most of the hardware things two hours away in Quelimane. He would ask the plumber for everything he was going to need for the week. He would make a list and Mike would drive to Quelimane and get it. Then the plumber would come up to him and say that he had forgotten something and needed more things! (They were never able to think ahead of all the things they were going to need.) Mike would just want to cry.

There was still no water to the house, and the roaches were still everywhere. You could take a shower downstairs, but the flying roaches were so bad, that the kids refused to take a shower - me too! We still hadn't unpacked our container (that we had packed 15 months earlier in North Carolina), because we didn't have the electrical plugs ready for us to plug in the appliances, etc. So for days, the houseworker cooked for us on the fire and if we needed a cold Coke or milk, we went down to the local shop to get one.

The first night we camped out in our new house, the kids were so upset. It began to dawn on them that we had moved to this god-forsaken house, and they had left their friends and pool and schools behind in Beira where we lived for language school. I was about ready to cry, because nothing I could say would make it better. I couldn't say that things were going to get better, because I had no idea what would happen to us in this new place. I didn't know if the house would ever be fixed and if they would ever have friends. I started to cry, but then stopped, and this silly song came to my head. There is that fun, upbeat Christian chorus which says, "What a Mighty God we Serve". That melody just came to my mind, and I began to sing, "What an ugly house we have, what an ugly house we have." The kids and I started laughing and when we got depressed about the house and our circumstances, we just started singing that song and it made us feel better!

Our "ugly" house

The only thing that seemed to help in those first few days and weeks was our trips to Quelimane to see the Dina family. They had three children that were near to the same age as our kids. They had a "normal" house - meaning they had all the furniture set up and nice meals, and toys; whereas our things were still in the container and we were camping out. We would take hot baths there and check our e-mail. We will never be able to fully convey to them our appreciation for the way they ministered to us while we were in Mocuba- especially those crucial first few months.

We knew that there were other missionaries in town, but we had not met any yet. We arrived in rainy season, and many of the missionaries would go home for Christmas, and stay away from December until February. They would miss the heat and rain, which made travel very difficult since so many roads were flooded. To help us meet people, we decided to go meet our neighbors. We went across the street to what looked like a nice Mozambican family. He ended up being the Commander of the Mocuba unit of the army. He had a nice house, TV and several children. He also had a broken down tank in front of his house that stayed there the whole time we lived there! It was a great thing for Timothy to climb on and pretend he was driving!

Tank across the street

So on the second day we were there, while Mike worked on the house, I took the kids over to meet our neighbors. They were very happy we came, and they offered us a Coke and asked us if we wanted to watch TV with them. My language skills were still not that great, so I guess they just decided we could watch TV together, since we weren't communicating too well! Since there were no TV channels at that time, you had to watch pre-recorded videos. So she sat all her kids down, plus many neighborhood kids who had wandered in her house to catch a glimpse of the new white people in town. I was thinking maybe it would be a cartoon, or something since there were probably 15 kids there. She put in a Brazilian soap opera, and in the very first few minutes, the couple in the video started undressing and then were completely naked and started kissing, and then on and on it went. It was pornography. I was about to die, and the lady in the house thought nothing of showing this to all these children! Timothy and Grace's eyes were as big as saucers. As politely as I could, I dismissed my kids and myself and thanked her for the visit. As I went home to my ugly house, the loneliness set it, but I knew it was for this reason that I had come - for moms like that that would show that to their children.

In time, the house was repaired. I had a nice indoor kitchen with cabinets and a sink. Water did get pumped up to the second floor and we could flush the toilet. Mike did install a hot water heater, and we had hot water. We could take a bath in the tub. We had burglar bars on every window and door. The inside was freshly painted and the windows fixed. We had light fixtures up and even ceiling fans with light kits. The bugs did leave. We got a cistern built outside, so that we could store up water, for the months when water was scarce and they only pumped out city water a few hours a day. We unpacked the container and we saw our things that we hadn't seen in 15 months. I put up curtains and the kids had a beautiful room.

We got the school desks made and the chalkboard up and we had a great schoolroom. I loved leaving my "house" and going downstairs to school. I left my chores, and was going to teach, and was not tempted to run inside to put in a load of clothes, or start lunch. We were at "school". In Beira, their school was called B.I.P.S., Beira International Primary School. To help them feel better and make the transition from Beira, I made a sign calling our new home school B.I.P.S.- Boone International Primary School! We planted some flowers and planted grass. In a few months time, you would have never believed it was the same house! When I began to feel sorry for the kids, I would remind myself that my kids went to a private, Christian, international school, with the teacher ratio of 2:1. Sounded pretty good.

We had packed everything we wanted to bring into that metal sea container. When it arrived by boat in the port of Quelimane, missionary John Dina had to go to help clear it through customs as we were in Beira at the time, 14 hours away. He graciously went to do that for us. Normally, the custom officials are not the kindest people on the earth! Many times, they expect you to unpack the entire thing, and many times they can charge you for items you bring into their country. When John went to the port, it was raining. They opened the container together, and a mop fell out and a framed picture. I can't remember packing this picture last, but somehow it got to the end and fell out. I am sure things definitely shifted during the long voyage. It is a picture of a boy holding a baseball bat, and Jesus is standing behind him with his arms around the boy, helping him bat. That is what fell out when the custom officials were there! He took one look at that picture and just told John to lock it back up-everything was fine! It was wonderful for us to see our possessions again. They had been on a boat for months, and then sat in a harbor. We didn't know if things would be ruined or not. As we began to unpack the things, we realized that nothing was broken! The glass china cabinet, the piano, all the pictures and dishes - nothing was broken! Timothy and Grace were so excited to see their things that had been stored for 15 months.

We got busy in our work and meeting the people. The church members came to visit us soon after we arrived and brought us a little black pig. He lived in our yard, since it was fenced in. It was quite a gift for them to give us. As they all sat inside and visited, Grace went around and painted all the women's fingernails. They talked about that for many years. We kept the pig for a while, but one day the city officials came and said that we could not have animals in a residential area. We would have to get rid of him, or face a stiff fine. We found a farm outside of town to keep him. We paid them to fatten him up, and we did kill him and eat him a year later!

There was so much poverty and hunger in our city. The day we killed this pig, people heard about it and started arriving at our gate with bowls and sacks. Our workers arrived and they had wheelbarrows and sacks also. They all wanted to take home the insides of that pig. They divided up every part of that pig. One person got the head and the feet, and the rest divided up all the organs and intestines. They did not let one part of that pig go uneaten.

The funny thing is that when I was at the Commander of the Army's house, across the street, he showed me his "farm" behind his house. I couldn't believe how, in the middle of the city, he was raising and keeping hundreds of pigs!   I am sure the city officials did not come to his house and tell him it was against the law.

Mike got involved in teaching TEE-Theological Education by Extension and his agricultural work. I got busy home schooling and getting to know the women of the church, and later would teach them how to read and write. Mainly, I would say, what we basically did was answer and respond to all the requests from the people that came to our gate. As soon as we moved in, our house became the thoroughfare of activity! By this time, we had turned our container into a Baptist bookstore. We had Sunday School materials, Bibles, hymnals and a lot of other literature. People came from the neighboring Baptist churches and from other denominations to get the literature. They seemed so hungry for it.

One of Mike's TEE class

Many times people would come to us for medical help. We would tell them we weren't doctors or nurses, but they trusted us to know how to help them and to give them medicine. We had to keep lots of medicine on hand - like painkillers, malaria medicine, worm medicine, and general first aid things. The ladies from the church would come with their sickly babies and I would always pray for them. Then I would ask about the symptoms. I had this book called, *Where there is no Doctor*, and when they would tell me the symptoms, I would look them up, and then try to diagnose them. It was scary many times since I had no medical training. I had heard of missionaries that had dispensed medicines, and then the baby died, and the missionaries got blamed. But in all our time there, no one ever came to tell me I had hurt their baby. They always would come back to say thank you. But it was still scary!

One time a lady came who had had triplets. There was no way she could nurse all three of them because she herself was malnourished. We had brought some baby formula with us that the churches had bought, and she had heard we had some. At that time, we were supplying the Mocuba hospital with baby formula, for mothers who couldn't nurse, or for children whose mothers died in childbirth. I will always be grateful to all those Baptists back home that donated the baby formula, plus a friend who got a company to donate a lot also. I am sure many babies lived that otherwise would not have.

We also brought eyeglasses with us, and churches would send us more when our supply would run low. People began to hear that we had glasses, and people came from far and near! We would give them a book and they would select the right pair for them by process of elimination. People would come to us and say, "Oh, I just want to be able to read the Bible again!" Again, we are grateful for all those that collected the glasses and paid the postage. Postage was a very expensive thing!

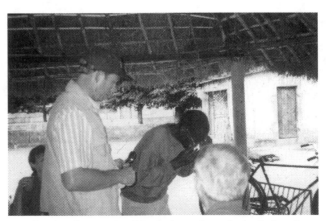

Mike and my Dad helping the church leader
choose his correct prescription

Many times when someone was at the gate, it was a pastor or leader of a church that Mike had not met yet. They heard there was a missionary in Mocuba, and many of them rode their bike for up to five hours to meet Mike and to ask him to come to their church. A church planting movement was happening in this part of Mozambique. This is when churches are started, and then on their own, they go out and start more churches. It had spread, until in our region, there were over 100 churches by the time we left. You can imagine how difficult it was to get to all of these places! Some of them could not be reached by car. It was always thrilling to meet a new pastor/leader that came to invite Mike to come to their church. So he began to mark his calendar with dates, trying to promise to go visit all the places that asked him.

When people came to see us, they would always have a gift. One of these church leaders - his name was Sabão - would ride his bike for six hours to reach our house. He was an older man too - probably in his 50's. And the bikes that they rode did not have gears. They were made in India and were very heavy. They had to climb hills and go up steep inclines to reach our house. He had brought us a chicken that he had tied upside down from his handlebars. It was hilarious watching that chicken try to walk after being tied upside down for 6 hours. We called him the "drunk chicken!" Sabão was coming to meet us and to ask us to come to his church. He was also coming for literature and for glasses. He also was asking for prayer for his daughter that they were expecting to die. The commitment of these men to ride their bikes so far was so inspiring. We did hear later that when he arrived home, his daughter had been healed.

Notice the live chicken tied to the handlebars that the church leader brought as a gift to us- he drove six hours to see us!

Chapter 7

THE PROVISIONS OF GOD

GOD PROVIDED so richly for us during those years in Mozambique. I have alluded to many instances so far, but I just want to elaborate on them. First of all, I must say that our sending organization, the International Mission Board provided for us so well. We are very grateful for the vehicle, medical insurance and house that they provided through the gifts and tithes of Baptists. We are so grateful that they allowed us, and all missionaries, to ship their household goods to the country where they would be serving. Not all boards do this, in fact, I would stay it is an exception, rather than the norm. The mission board also provided school books for Timothy and Grace. We had a dear missionary friend in Mozambique and she and her family were struggling financially. Her organization did not provide school books for her children, which were the same ages as Timothy and Grace. So, many times, she would come over to our house on the weekends and she would copy down the math problems and worksheets from Timothy and Grace's books for her kids to use in the following week. She would sit there and copy for hours and hours. After that, I did not take the expensive books for granted.

Even in transit to Mozambique that first time, we saw God's hand. I had a carry-on bag that was full of my medicine for those first years – medicine for every possible ailment that we thought we may have! The contents of that bag alone was very expensive. As we were boarding our flight, they told us that the overhead cabinet space was full, and they began to take carry-on bags from people and put them in the underneath checked baggage. So they took my bag of medicine, much to my displeasure! They told us they would check all our bags all the way to Zimbabwe; that we would not have to collect them in Germany on our first lay-over. As we were hurrying through the Frankfurt airport at our first stop, we happened to pass by the luggage conveyor belts. As I just happened to glance at one of them, I saw this lone green bag circling all alone. I just stared at it a minute, and thought, "Wow, that looks so much like my medicine suitcase." Something told me to inspect it further, and low and behold it was my medicine bag! None of our other eight trunks were there, because they were being checked all the way through! We saw His kindness and provision for us from the very start.

We are also grateful how God protected our possessions while they were in transit. I brought my piano and my glass china cabinet, and until this day, ten years later, they are in excellent condition. We did lose a few things to theft during our second move. We grieved about one of Mike's grandmothers quilts being stolen and other things, but I guess it is amazing more things weren't stolen. My piano should be ruined because of all the humidity and the 29 months that it has sat in a shipping container, between our 2 moves. During the last move from Mozambique to South Africa, when the forklight picked up the container to ship it, it punched holes on either side. During the 12 months it sat outside in storage, several things got ruined on the inside because of the rain. My piano was fine, but I lost a lot of my precious music and other valuable papers – many of my Dad's sermons. But we praise God that more things weren't ruined by the rain. It was wonderful that my piano didn't get ruined - again, it should have been! But God has been so faithful to protect our possession from theft and from the elements.

Our waterbed mattress was ruined on that second move as well. It got many holes in the bed and we were unable to use it. On Friday in South Africa, it is trash day. If you have something to discard that is large and won't fit in your trashcan, you put it on the road in front of your house. So when we saw the waterbed mattress was ruined and had unsuccessful attempts in reparing it, we put it on the road. Before the trash men came, we heard our doorbell ring and a man asked us if he could have the mattress. He lived in a tin shack and said that he was going to put the mattress on his roof to keep the rain from coming in - it would make a nice tarp. So somewhere in Cape Town our waterbed is someone's roof!

We are grateful for these material possessions, but the main way we feel God cared for us was through the other missionaries and internationals that lived in Mocuba. Because there was very little to do in the city - in terms of restaurants, movies, a pool, shopping, etc.- going to each others' houses became a blessing and a respite. There were many missionaries in Mocuba with all different kinds of jobs and from different organizations. Because we had electricity in Mocuba, each of us would kind of use Mocuba as a base from which to travel to the rural areas in our work.

Soon after we moved there, we began to feel the need to have an English fellowship, like the one we had in Beira. The plan was for everyone to go to their African churches in the morning, and then on Sunday evening, they would gather at our house for an English worship service. Our house had an open plan with a great room, so it was perfect for the fellowship. I had my piano there also. So we invited all the missionaries and other internationals and also opened it up to any Mozambicans that wanted to use their English, or learn English. We made a roster and took turns preaching and leading the music. In time, we purchased hymnbooks from South Africa and used them. After the praise and worship time, the children went off to Sunday School, and we took turns teaching the children. The separate room under our house was perfect for that, because we could not even hear them when they were under there.

Many of the other missionary families also had to home school their children. Each mother seemed to be gifted in a different way, and we decided to form a home schooling group for the afternoons. We each spoke a different language for our schoolwork, but in the afternoons, we could come together in English for the extra curricular activities. It was amazing that in this very small village, families were there home schooling in Afrikaans, Dutch and French! On Mondays, the girls would go to one home, and have a Girl's Club. They did crafts and hikes and other activities. The boys would play baseball on Mondays. On Tuesdays, they would have art lessons. On Wednesdays, the boys would do baseball again. On Thursdays, they would all have drama and afterwards, the girls would have Christian interpretive dance. On Fridays, I would teach all of them music.

God so provided through these different families. When one would leave, another would come in their place that also had skills they were willing to share. Three different missionary ladies taught my kids art in the 4 ½ years we were in Mocuba. Another time, a man taught them recorder lessons for a while. Another year, we found a young Mozambican man that spoke beautiful English, and he taught Timothy guitar lessons. It was quite amazing to find a young man like this that could speak English, as this was quite rare.

A very special missionary with Operation Mobilization was Liz West. She was from South Africa and had been a missionary for many years. She worked with all the children in the area of drama and dance. These dramas and Christian dances were then presented in the English fellowship on Sunday nights. Sometimes once a month, and other times once a quarter, the children would lead the entire service. They would choose the hymns and present the message through the dramas and songs. They did Christmas plays as well each year. She would also have them spend the night at her house and would play Bible trivia games with them.

There were six little girls all about Grace's age. Liz taught them a special song about God loving all the children of the world. She got each of them to make a flag from their country, and they did an interpretive dance using those flags to that song. The six girls were from South Africa, Holland, Burundi, Mozambique, Kenya, and of course, Grace from America. What a special night to have several nations of the world represented in my living room!

Grace and two friends doing an interpretive dance during the English fellowship at our house.

In this group were many talented people. One man had brought his lovely antique pipe organ with him from Holland and we would go to his house for organ recitals- in the middle of war-torn Mozambique! Another lady was a very talented hair-stylist- having worked in a hair salon in Sun City (the Las Vegas of South Africa) before she was saved. She was willing to cut all the internationals' hair whenever we needed it! I had packed many home perms kits, with instructions for Mike on how to give me a perm. But when we were packing, we didn't know God would provide us with a professional hair stylist in our town! Mike never had to give me a perm. In this group, from time to time, there were several that were doctors, others were nurses, and one was a trained veterinarian.

Our nextdoor neighbors were the Agenbag family from South Africa. They had six children. Our yards had a small fence that separated them. To make it easier for the children to go back and forth, we each put a stepping-stone so that the children could easily climb over the fence. They are such a godly family and we learned so much from them. We would pray together and they helped us through many a rough time. Our children were inseparable. They would get together first thing in the morning and play together until it was dark. The beautiful thing was that one of their daughters was 13 at the time, but she was so kind to Timothy who was eight. They would climb trees and at one stage put on a circus where they did pyramids and tricks with the swing, and even served popcorn to the parents in the audience.

Not only did God provide for us through these friends, but also through the relationships we made with the Mozambicans. They were the reason we were there! We had round the clock guards that stayed at our house, plus a houseworker. So at any given time, two Mozambicans would be with us. We became very close to them. Whenever we had to fire one of them, for one reason or another, it would affect us deeply, since they had each become part of the family. One time, one of them started drinking, and he kept coming to work drunk. He was the night guard, and he was sleeping all night long. So when he wouldn't stop, we had to fire him. But otherwise, we had guards that worked with us for years. When Grace was playing at someone else's house, I would ask the guard to go and pick her up on his bicycle. It would be getting dark, and I was busy cooking supper. I have such fond memories of a little blond girl on the back of those Mozambican bikes with such trusted, wonderful men. They would go, rain or shine. They had raincoats, and if it had started raining while she was gone, they would take her raincoat, and sometimes even drive with one hand on the handlebars, and another holding an umbrella over Grace! (You may wonder why I wouldn't go pick up Grace in the car. Well, many times, Mike was away. Mike had to travel such long distances to visit the many churches. We only had one car, and sometimes he was gone from home three to four days a week.)

One day, we were having a particularly rough time pulling one of Grace's teeth. It was just hanging there and her mouth was bleeding. I tried to help, but she wouldn't let me - an occasion like this called for the strength of a man! She cried for Mike, but I reminded her that he was out of town ministering for the day. She was crying hysterically. Then without even thinking, she called for Antunus, the day guard. He took her in his lap and in his arms and pulled her tooth. She immediately stopped crying! That was how close we were to these guys. They were like family!

Because there was no commercially prepared dog food to buy where we lived, the guard would cook the dog's rice and dried fish each night. So, many nights we talked through the screen door (so the mosquitoes wouldn't get in), while they cooked the dog's food.

We had some great conversations, and can honestly say they were more than our workers, they were our friends. Antunus was our favorite guard/worker. During one year that he worked for us, he slowly got to where he could hardly walk. We sent him to the clinic, and then to the provincial hospital, but no one could find out why he just suddenly was almost paralyzed. One Mozambican doctor diagnosed him with TB of the back, and he was put in the awful TB ward with everyone coughing, and many even dying. He was in there for months on end. We would visit him and pray for him faithfully. He couldn't walk for over a year. We kept praying for a miracle. Without medical insurance, or disability insurance, if he didn't work, his family wouldn't make it. We prayed and prayed and told him a miracle was going to happen. All of the sudden, after one year of not being able to walk, he just got up and walked and was fine again. I will never forget the look on our faces when he came driving up into our yard on his bike. What a miracle!

The pastor of our church in Mocuba was a trained nurse. One day while Mike was helping put the roof on the new church building, one of those tin sheets slit Mike's leg open. He knew he would need stitches, but we were all terrified of the local hospital! I had brought stitches from the states for times like this. The hospital was not clean- they shared needles and it was so dirty. So we sent one of our guards to call our pastor and he came quickly to our house. I had the stitches, and he brought some local anesthesia. Mike leaned back in our Lazy-Boy recliner, and elevated his hurt leg on the footrest of the Lazy-Boy. The anesthesia was topical, and thus there was still great pain as he sewed up his leg! Mike about passed out with the pain, but the wound did close nicely and heal!

Mike during "surgery" on our couch!

We did love the people in all the Baptist churches, especially the ones from our home church there in Mocuba. I met with the ladies each Saturday morning and we would sing and pray, and then we would always go visiting together. I loved those ladies. I would be the only white person walking through their villages, and I never felt awkward or out of place. I felt more at home with these ladies walking through the villages than I would anywhere else. We would go visit the sick, and women that were no longer coming to church, and after a funeral, we would visit the family of the bereaved. These were precious times. They treated us like royalty. Mozambicans came to our gate all day long and I know they knew we cared from them.

God also provided for us by sending us IMB missionary colleagues in the last year we were there. We had put in a job request for an agricultural evangelist to help Mike. A young couple from Texas, Sam and Kylah Clark-Goff, accepted the job and they were such a blessing to us. Sam was a missionary kid from South America, and due to his Spanish background, he picked up Portuguese unbelievably fast. He was such a help in the agricultural side to Mike's ministry. Kylah was a trained teacher and she helped me in home schooling Timothy and Grace in some subjects. They became dear friends and we will always know that God sent them!

These are verses that reminded me of His power and provisions:

His divine power has given us everything we need for life and godliness through our knowledge of him who called us by his own glory and goodness. (2 Peter 1:3)

May the God of peace, who through the blood of the eternal covenant brought back from the dead our Lord Jesus, that great Shepherd of the sheep, equip you with everything good for doing his will, and may he work in us what is pleasing to him, through Jesus Christ, to whom be glory for ever and ever. (Hebrews 13:20-21)

Through the provisions I have mentioned in this chapter, God equipped us with all we needed to do His will, which was to minister daily to the Mozambican people.

Chapter 8

THE MIRACLES

H ERE ARE 10 short stories of miracles that God performed. The definition of the word "miracle" is: an extraordinary event manifesting a supernatural work of God. So He gets all the glory for these wonderful stories that follow!

Miracle #1 - To Catch a Radio Thief

One morning at 3:30 a.m. our night guard called to us, saying that someone had stolen something from our house. In our grogginess, we looked outside and saw a policeman with another man that had his arms tied. Mike went out and heard the story:

Mike had a very special radio, called a Worldspace satellite radio. Since we didn't have a satellite disc for the TV, this was our only connection with the outside world. We could pick up CNN and BBC, and even the Larry King Live show!! It sat on top of a bookcase near a window- the best place to pick up reception. We had burglar bars up and screens, and didn't feel it was a problem. That night, the heat was unbearable, and we had left a few windows open to allow for some air to circulate. (In hindsight, we shouldn't have left open the window by the radio). The neighbors were constantly watching us and knew everything about us, and for sure, they had seen the radio as they looked in through the windows.

Some smart thief with a knife, cut open the screen, reached his hand in, and stole Mike's new radio through the burglar bars. He did all this despite the fact that we had a wall around our house, two guards, and two dogs! The thief then tried to sell it at a bar down the street from us- it was open at 3:00 a.m.! The owner of the bar said he would not buy it unless the man had a receipt. The thief confessed that he had just stolen it from our house, and the owner dragged him to the police station (it was a small town). The night policeman knew us and wanted to return the radio.

So at 3:30 a.m., the police came to tell us what had happened and to ask Mike what he wanted to do with the thief. The thief had been tied up with the cord from the radio- that was the only rope they had. To get the radio back, Mike walked a mile to the station with the police officer, one of our guards and the tied-up thief. The man had already been beaten, but the officers promised us they had not done the "normal" beating- they were waiting for permission from Mike as to how many beatings to do.

Mike begged them not to beat him anymore, but asked them to just put him to work- cleaning up trash in the city, or putting in dirt to cover up some of the potholes. (We are not talking about potholes like you know them; we are talking about holes big enough to swallow your car!) They agreed to this. Mike went the next day to visit the man in jail, and shared the Gospel with him.

The police at the station were very curious about this "thing" - the radio. (They probably would have stolen it, had they known how it worked, but they couldn't get it turned on!) They thought it was a way for us to "talk" to the people in America. They were very suspicious of outsiders and assumed we were all spies. When Mike explained that it was a satellite radio, they were totally confused, since their local radios didn't look like this one. They asked Mike, what was a satellite? Mike said, "You know those things that float around the world, and thus broadcast news from other places." Then they were really confused. I can just see Mike now in his bed shorts trying to speak a foreign language in a police station at 4 a.m., beside a thief tied up in his radio cord!

This is a wild story, but let me share some neat things that show God was working a miracle out.

1. In a very corrupt country, even the police rarely give back stolen goods. Since they are overworked and underpaid, they often help themselves to recovered stolen goods. It would not have been normal for the owner of the bar and the policeman to return the

radio. But through the eyeglass ministry, this policeman had been to our house and received some glasses. When he found out which house had been robbed from, he said immediately that those (us) are good people, and that the radio must thus be returned! This was unheard of and is a miracle!

2.   We also praise God that our children are sound sleepers. It would have been very traumatic for the children to have heard the man being beaten outside their window, before we asked the policemen to stop.

3.   Another thing is that we would always close all the windows upstairs where we slept, since the air conditioners were on. We had never accidentally left a window open upstairs, because that would not keep the cold air in! When our windows are shut and the AC is on, it is impossible for anyone to get our attention during the night. Since we had big gates for security in front of the doors downstairs, no one could get to our front door to knock, and even if they could, we wouldn't have heard them. We were so tired on this night that we went to bed with the AC on and one of the windows in our room open! Therefore we heard the guard when he called us at 3:30. This is another miracle. Had we not heard the call, the radio would have been a goner by daybreak.

4.   Five years later, we still have the radio and it still keeps us up to date with what is happening in the world. These radios have become very expensive, and would have been hard to replace.

A final cultural note- in their animist beliefs, (where they worship their ancestors), magic and superstition play a huge part. Before a thief steals, they go to the witch doctor, and he/she gives him something to make him " invisible", so they can steal without the guards or anyone seeing them. I guess the thief will think it worked, since he did it without the guards or dogs noticing. Just an interesting cultural fact!

Miracle #2 – The Glasses and Medicine Miracle

We were on a family vacation in northern Mozambique at the Island of Mozambique. It is called the Ilha, and is a world heritage site. You get to it by crossing a huge bridge and you see such fascinating things - a fort, old cathedral, museums, etc. Portuguese explorers had landed in this region in the 15th century. This island had remained the capital of Portugal's east African colony until the late 19th century. So the governor had a palace there, and it is full of valuable relics.   We stopped to visit some of these places, yet had our suitcases in the cab of our pickup truck because we were going to a hotel that night. (We could have checked in earlier, so as not to be riding around with our suitcases, but we felt they were safer with us, since there are even robberies from the hotels.) The cab was locked and even had an alarm and we were never far from the car- we drove from site to site, even though one could easily have walked. But it was disconcerting to see the bands of young boys that would surround the tourists at every turn. Everywhere we walked, they surrounded us and were begging. They were really quite scary, even though they were young.

We were just going to stay for a few nights, so we only had our essentials with us - some changes of clothes, medicine, toiletries, camera and our Bibles. I have terrible migraines, and the only medicines I have that treat them, are from the USA. So I could not replace them easily. Most medicines had to be hand carried by a person traveling from the USA to Mozambique, as medicines would easily be stolen through the mail. I had taken all of it with me, as sometimes I can have a migraine almost every day of the week.   It wasn't a tremendous quantity, as we were having visitors from the states soon that were going to bring me some more. So I was nearing the end of my supply, but it was still a lot of medicine.

Another thing you must know about me, is that I have very poor vision. I have worn glasses since Second Grade, and can literally see nothing when I don't have my contacts or glasses on. I was wearing my contacts as we toured the Island, and my glasses were safely in my suitcase in the cab. My contacts are the hard type, since I have an astigmatism and can't wear the soft kind. So after about eight hours in the dry, hot, dusty Mozambique weather, I have to take them out, because my eyes would be killing me by that time. (Oh, what we do for vanities sake!) So at about 5:00 each day I have had enough and I take them out and put on my glasses.

So after touring for a few hours, I needed to get something from my suitcase in the canopy of our truck. As I opened my suitcase, I saw that it was completely empty, except for my Bible. The thieves had not touched my husband's or my two children's bags. They were fine. A small boy had somehow slid open the window on the canopy, and had carefully opened my bag, and one by one, taken everything in my suitcase through the burglar bars, except for my Bible. My glasses were gone, my clothes, my medicine, and my camera. I was stunned beyond belief. It must have been a very small boy, because the window could only be slid to a small opening. As I thought of my glasses and my medicine being gone, I wept and wept and could not stop crying.

We left the island immediately and drove several hours to a missionary's home. We did not even go to the hotel- our vacation was over in my book! They didn't know we were coming and were shocked to see us, but very gracious to take us in, since we were far from home. We told them the story, and they were very kind to us and fed us supper. I retired early and went to my room and was alone with God. I was angrier than I have ever been. I screamed out to God that He promised to be with me and care for me, and that He had not. I told Him that He said in His word, that "His grace is sufficient for me", and I told Him, that at this time, I felt that was not true. I just kept crying out, "Why, why, why, did you allow my glasses and medicine to be stolen?" In a more modern country, you would just go and get it replaced, but we were in such a remote place. There were no ophthalmologists or opticians, and none of this medicine. Without that medicine, when I got a headache, I would have to be in bed for two to three days, in great pain. All I could do was envision the future, and what would happen to me. There is no way I can convey to you the panic that I felt.

I was tired of being alone, and went out to the living room where the missionaries and the rest of my family was sitting. They could see I was deeply upset. The missionary, Dianne, had an idea. She collected old glasses from people in the states, and distributed them to the people in Mozambique, like we did. She told me me to look through the box and try them on one by one to find my exact prescription. I must say the box she gave me had very old glasses in it, even broken pairs. She kept telling me to do it, but I just knew that there would never be a pair with my exact strength. One by one I tried on these old glasses in the crumpled box. The third pair I picked up was a cute pink pair in very good shape, and can you believe, they were the exact strength I needed. (And God even made them to be a nice pair!) I was so shocked I couldn't speak. I wore those glasses for the next 3-4 months until the visitors were coming and could bring me some more. I still have them to this day as a vivid memory of God's goodness to me.

The second miracle is that in that time, before I got the medicine replaced, I did not have *one* headache. For that period that I didn't have any medicine, until I could get more, God completely healed me. As I have said before, sometimes I would have four to five migraine headaches a week! When more medicine was delivered, I started having the headaches again. Our God knew where we were, and He knew I had no medicine and He provided. He is Jehovah Jireh.

Miracle #3 - My Trip Home from Johannesburg

We were living in northern Mozambique at the time. To get to Johannesburg by car, it took four days. To go by air, it first meant driving the two-hour drive to the Quelimane airport, then a two-hour flight to the capital, and then another flight into South Africa. There aren't daily flights into South Africa, so you have to really plan ahead and be flexible!

We had been to Johannesburg a few months earlier having our annual medical check-ups. The gynecologist found some pre-cancerous cells in a test she did on me, and requested that I come back in six months for a re-check. So with much fear and trepidation, I left Mike and the kids in Mocuba, and flew alone to South Africa for the test. My kids were still quite young, and it was hard for me to leave them. When I got there, the test came out fine and there was no need for surgery or anything. When I got the results back, I was ready to go home! Then came the problem of booking my flight back, since the planes only fly on certain days. And if I had missed it, it could be several days before I could fly.

The Mozambican airline is called LAM - the acronym of three Portuguese words. The internationals who use it also jokingly refer to it as "Late and Maybe"! I went to the Johannesburg airport and tried to book a ticket at the LAM office. Believe it or not, they were not computerized at the time, and just had an old schedule on a piece of paper. They could not tell me when a flight would be going to Quelimane. They told me I must fly to the capital city, Maputo, and just wait there until a flight was going to Quelimane. That alone took great faith, because I knew no one in Maputo. Who would pick me up from the airport, and where would I wait for the few days until a plane was going to Quelimane? In hindsight, I should have gone back to the hotel and called Maputo and found out the schedule, since the LAM office in Johannesburg didn't know. A part of me was saying, " Amy, you are a fool to buy that ticket, not knowing anything"! But God quietly spoke to me as I was reluctantly buying my ticket to Maputo. He told me, "You will be home today; you will see your children today."

In a few hours, I was on my way to Maputo, dreading what would happen to me when I got there. As I got on this plane, they told us that their LAM plane was broken, and they had borrowed another plane, and it was called "Lucky Airlines". I was scared to death! When I got on the plane, I noticed that it was filled with athletes of some kind, all in their uniforms. I heard them all talking about their tournament, etc.

As soon as I got on the plane, the flight attendant came over the intercom welcoming us and showing us the safety features on this "Lucky" plane. She then explained to us all that on the flight was a soccer team on its way to a tournament in Quelimane! She explained that they would just be touching down in Maputo for a few minutes to let some passengers off, and then the plane would be continuing on to Quelimane. I was home in a few hours!

It is "Lucky" that we got there, because the plane was in bad shape. When we landed in Quelimane, part of the ceiling fell down on our heads as we landed. But I was too busy praising God to worry about that! My family wasn't even there to meet me, as I hadn't had time to tell them I was coming. But other missionaries picked me up and my family was there in two hours!

Miracle #4- A Doctor from Holland

While living in Mozambique, Timothy had malaria five times. Most of the time, he was able to swallow and keep the medicine down that one must take to be healed. Many people die from malaria, and it is usually because they do not get the medicine quickly enough. But this particular time, he was vomiting so much that he was not able to keep any medicine down. We began to see he was going down hill very fast and we needed to get him an injection. (We kept all this medicine on hand- even needles and syringes!)   But neither of us knew how to give shots (I sure should have learned that before going to Mozambique!). I had a friend from Holland that was a nurse living in our city, and she came over from time to time when we needed some medical help or advice. (Later in our stay in Mocuba, our pastor, who was a trained nurse, would help us, but he was away at medical school at this time far from Mocuba.)   I knew my nurse friend, Remke, was out of town. She told us she was going to Malawi to the airport to pick up someone and would be back later in the week. (Most of our visitors flying in to see people in Mocuba would fly into the international airport in Malawi - six hours away.) So I knew I couldn't call her, because I knew she was gone.

We were really getting worried about how we were going to give Timothy this shot. Malaria is a very scary disease, and many children worldwide die from it. At this point, we didn't have phones, so when we needed to get a message to someone, we would send our guards on their bicycle with a note, and they were a big help to us, getting word to whomever we needed to communicate with. So just out of the blue, I asked our night guard to go to Remke's house, just to see if, by chance, she had come home early from the airport. To my surprise, he came back to say she was home! I couldn't believe it. In a few minutes, she came over with a very tall man besides her - I presumed the person she had gone to the airport to get. She began to tell me that this was her father, a doctor from Holland! She told me that his flight arrived early, and that they had decided to come straight home from the airport, rather than spend a few nights in Malawi, as she had originally told me.

The kind doctor went upstairs where Timothy was lying. He got on his knees beside Timothy's bed and reached for Timothy's hand. He introduced himself as Dr. Oosterhuis and stroked his feverish face. I will never forget the kindness and compassion of this man. He was directly from God! He gave Timothy the shot, prayed with him and, because they were so tired from their journey, left.

Later that night, the toll of the day and his sickness really began to affect me. I was deeply troubled by seeing my children sick with malaria. I cried out to God and said, "I can't do this anymore. We have to move to an easier place. I can't stand my kids being sick. Why, why, why?" Satan can make one feel very guilty for taking your children to Africa where they have these diseases that most other children will never have to face. As I was so distressed, I heard God speak to me in a clear, audible voice. He said to me, "I sent you a doctor from Holland, the minute you needed one, what else do you want?" I was so humbled by this, that yes, God was our healer and our provider, and He had the power to provide anything we needed.

Miracle #5- Transformer on Fire

Each night during the intense heat, we would run our window air conditioning units. Many times the power would not be strong enough to run all three of them - ours, and then one in Timothy's room, and one in Grace's. So usually one of us would sleep in the heat, (or Timothy would come and sleep on our floor, because usually his wouldn't work.) To run the air conditioners, you had to use a transformer, to convert the voltage from 110 (in America) to the 220 volts needed in Africa. It is just a small electrical box that the AC would be plugged into, and then the transformer would be plugged into the wall.

You could sleep well when the AC was on. Its low, rumbling noise was just what we needed to sleep well, and it was cool, so you weren't uncomfortable and miserable with the high temperature and humidity. Mike and I both are heavy sleepers. We usually don't wake up, once we fall asleep. One night, as our AC was running, the transformer caught on fire. It could have been very dangerous and burnt our house down. For some reason, just as it caught on fire, I woke up. It didn't smell, or make a noise, I just woke up and happened to look down and saw that the black transformer was now red! I realized the danger, but didn't know if it would explode or not. I woke Mike up, and with potholders from the kitchen, he carried the blazing red transformer outside. He acted so quickly, and thought so clearly for a man that was asleep. Only after it was over did we realize the true danger of that situation. If God had not woken me up, there is no telling what would have happened. We serve an amazing God!

Miracle #6 - The Pirate Suit

When Timothy was a small boy, he just loved the whole pirate thing. He had books about them, movies, and a costume. Whenever he was given paper to draw a picture, he drew pirates! He had this neat pirate suit. It was red velvet, with a white frilly collar, and black pants. He loved to wear it around the house and of course to Trick-or-Treat. When we got ready to pack to come to Africa, I decided that we needed to leave the pirate suit in America. We knew he would grow out of it soon, and we also knew the African children would not understand why the missionary kid had this funny suit on! He would have been quite upset, had we told him, so we just gave it to the Salvation Army thift shop and hoped he would forget about it.

The children were both having a hard time packing up their things to go to Africa. We could only take a few favorite things with us for the first year, but would then get our container with all our belongings after we finished language school in a year. It would have been too expensive to have unpacked all our things for that first year, and to then repack them and ship them to our permanent assignment. So as we packed the container, we kept telling the kids, "Don't worry, we are not leaving anything behind. One day, you will see all your things again." But it is a pretty tough thing for a child to only have one footlocker for their favorite things, and then to have to pack all their other things away for a year. They kept asking us if we were sure they were going to see all their things again. They wanted us to promise!

So Timothy never mentioned his pirate suit, until one day, after we had finished language school, and had unpacked all our things, he began to look for it. At first, I was tempted to lie to him that it was here, and surely we will find it in some box soon! But then I realized I must tell the truth. So I told him the whole story about leaving it behind, since it would be getting too small for him, etc. He was quite upset with me.

A few days later, we went to the clothing market there in Mocuba. It was a fun place to walk around. The American government and other countries sent free clothing to Africa in those huge white mailing sacks. The Mozambicans would take these clothes and then sell them at the clothing market. It took up a whole street -

little bamboo stalls with a few clothes in each shelter - hanging on little pieces of wood tied up with strings. One "shop" would have jeans, the next blankets, the next children's clothes, the next dresses, and the next tee-shirts, etc. They had quite a business going! I loved it because it was almost like going to a consignment shop- sometimes you found some beautiful things in great shape- even name brand clothes! We would go just to see what interesting things we could find, since most of them were from America- so you could find a Yankees shirt and McDonald uniforms and things like that.

On this particular day, we were looking through the children's "shop". Lo and behold, on a little wooden stick, hung a pirate suit exactly like the one that I had left behind in America! Timothy screamed out when he saw it, and of course, we bought it! I have kept it to this day, to remind Timothy and myself that God cares about everything. It may be a small thing to you, but to a six-year-old boy, who was mad at his mom, it was *huge*!

Miracle #7- Lead in the Eye

One day Mike was welding. He always had to fix things himself. He always wore the protective goggles when he would weld. He was almost finished, and had taken the goggles off and gone inside to get something. When he came out, he just had about a minute left of welding, and he had left the goggles inside. So he just decided since he was almost done, he would do it without the protective goggles. Well, immediately, a small piece of lead got in his eye. It was small, but was big enough that you could see it and it had to be removed. In a developed country, one would immediately go to the Emergency Room, but we didn't have one of those. So we had to go into overdrive and decide how to handle this one!

At the time this happened, we had a missionary friend from Canada staying with us. She is a trained nurse and was very helpful to us as we worked through what we would need to do. She said the first thing, was that we needed anesthetic for the eye. I knew they would not have that at the Mocuba hospital; they just had aspirin and malaria medicine! Whatever was wrong with you, you got one or the other! So I called our missionary friends in the city two hours away. They had a provincial hospital, and could possibly get this anesthetic.   I called them, and they were happy to go the hospital and try to get it; they had connections there and would do that for us. But the miracle is that John, the missionary we called, was on his way to Mocuba the minute we called! He had scheduled a meeting with a pastor near us, and we didn't know he was coming, but he was on his way and would pass our house. Otherwise, we were going to have to send one of our guards to travel by taxi to Quelimane, get the medicine, and then drive two hours back- so it would have been at least six hours before we would have the needed anesthetic. We could not believe John was on his way to our house. We serve a miracle working God!

The next dilemma was who was going to get the lead out. We had a trained doctor from Nigeria that lived in our town at this time. The problem is that he had never practiced as a doctor. He just had the education, and had come to Mozambique to set up rural clinics. He was an administrator, and did not know how to treat patients, especially not how to do what we needed him to do.

But nevertheless we went to his house, and he was out of town! We really did not know how this was going to work out. In the back of our minds, when we needed medical care, we always wondered if we were going to have to make that difficult trip to Malawi to the hospital - six hours on a dirt road, plus a border crossing.   But the beautiful thing is that in the two hours that it took for the anesthetic to come, the doctor arrived home! When we asked him to please come, he refused, saying he had no idea how to do what we were asking him to do. Finally, the nurse that was staying with us went to him, and told him that she knew a little bit and they could pool their ignorance, and that she would be there to help him!

So the medicine arrived, and the doctor came, and the nurse was ready. They deadened the eye and were able to get it out with some tweezers, and Mike had no residual effects from this. God is sovereign, over all things!

Miracle #8- Car Breaking Down

One day, I was driving our truck to Quelimane to the airport to pick up Nancy, the missionary nurse from Beira that was coming to stay with us for two weeks. She was going to be doing some teaching about AIDS and other health issues in the churches. She had never been to Mocuba, and we were very excited about her two weeks with us. We had made a friendship with her during that first year when we were in language school, and had missed her. We were very happy could see our house and we could work together in the churches. As we were coming back from the airport, our truck began losing power, and then it just stopped. We were absolutely in the middle of nowhere! On the two-hour trip to Quelimane from Mocuba, the first 45 minutes is paved and the last 45 minutes is paved and the 30 minutes in the middle is dirt. We were on the dirt part. The heat was unbearable and we had no food or water, and of course, no cell phone. It was Nancy, my daughter Grace, a friend named Liz, my house worker Simões and me.

As soon as it happened, I just began to laugh. The others in the car wondered why I was laughing at this terrible situation! I just said that I couldn't wait to see how God was going to get us out of this one! Somehow we had to get word back to Mike about our situation, and then someone would have to be willing to come and tow us. There were no tow trucks in Mocuba! For what seemed like hours, not a soul passed us on this deserted road. Our plan was to flag down the first taxi and ask them to take a message to Mike for him to please find someone to come and tow us. After several hours, we really began to worry since it was about 100 degrees, and we had no water or food. Finally after two hours, a taxi passed us. Liz agreed to flag them down and ask them to take her to Mocuba, and she would go and find Mike. She got on the taxi and off she went.

Another long time passed and I realized Grace must get out of this heat and get some water. So we decided we must flag down the next taxi that passed and pay them to take Nancy and Grace to our house. Now Mozambican taxis are like most public transport in developing countries. Goats and chickens are tied on top, as well as bikes and if they hold 15 people, they will have 30 people in there. Most of them look like they won't make it another mile - they are so banged up. So I dreaded sending my daughter and Nancy on one of these, but I had no choice. But the taxi that came by next was quite a nice taxi - it actually had room for two more people, and it looked like a new mini-van. I couldn't believe it!

Nancy had never been to our house, so she had no idea where she was going. So I explained to the taxi driver where we lived and that they must drop her and Grace at that house. Grace was the only one that knew the house, and she would have to take the taxi there! It takes a lot of trust to send one's five-year old daughter and friend on a taxi, having no idea who the driver is, and if he would really take them to the house.

When they left, it was just my worker and me. I was so thankful I had brought him along. A male presence provided me with a great deal of comfort and protection. More time passed and I was starving and thirsty. I knew by the time Liz and the others got to Mocuba, and found Mike, and by the time he found a car that would come tow us, several hours would have passed. So I tried to be calm and pray and wait!

There were very few people around us where we stopped. Across from where we broke down, were two huts and lots of farms. All of a sudden, this African man came up to me, saying "Irmã Amy, Irmã Amy" (sister Amy). He came from one of the huts across the street. My houseworker immediately came to step in front of me to protect me. I was so touched by his concern. I asked him his name and how he knew me. I had never traveled specifically to this part of Mozambique, other than just passing through. He told me that he had just gotten out of prison and that I had ministered to him in the Mocuba jail! (This made my houseworker really stand in front of me to protect me, when he found out this guy was a former prisoner!) I went weekly to the jail and held a worship service for the prisoners. Then many of them did a Bible course called Bible Way Correspondence Course, which is a 10-book study that they do on their own. After they finished the book, they took an exam, which I graded. He had been enrolled in this Bible Way course when he was in prison in Mocuba. After seeing us, he brought me oranges - a whole basket of them. This was great for my hunger, as well as my thirst. I could never have drunk any water, had he offered it to me, because it would not have been purified. So the oranges were great to rehydrate me. Just as we were eating the oranges, another car passed. It was our friends from England that were our neighbors in Mocuba. They had been out of town and were returning. They saw our situation, and that it was getting dark, and asked if they could tow us. We told them that hopefully Mike was on his way, but they could start towing us in the meantime. Since there was just one road from Mocuba to Quelimane, Mike couldn't miss us. They towed us, and then in a little while, we saw Mike coming to get us. He was in a Land Rover that belonged to a Dutch missionary.

The reason it had taken Mike so long to come and get us, was that he had not been home when Grace, Nancy and Liz arrived! But when he did get home and heard their story, he immediately came to get us.

In this story, many miracles took place. The first is that Liz and Nancy and Grace were able to safely travel by public transport back to Mocuba. It is a miracle that Nancy and Grace could find our house, even though Nancy had never been there. It was wonderful I had taken the house worker with me. It was amazing that in the middle of nowhere, a former prisoner knew me, and kindly shared his oranges with us. Then that the family from England passed us, so that they could begin towing us so we could all get home before dark. What a marvelous God!

Miracle #9- Rabies Shot

One day, a stray dog bit Timothy while he was at a mission compound where a group of other missionaries lived. Most of the dogs in our town had not been given a rabies injection. The dog looked very sickly, and we were worried. The first symptoms of rabies appear from ten days to up to a few weeks after the bite. Treatment must begin before the first signs of the sickness appear. Once the sickness begins, no treatment known to medical science can save the person's life. We did not have the necessary injections, so we knew we needed to make plans to travel to get them. We could probably get them in the city two hours from us, Quelimane, and if not, we would need to travel the six hours to Malawi.

After the dog bit Timothy, I went to visit the only doctor in town at the time, a Nigerian, named Victor. He was a very good doctor and we knew we could trust his advice. He told us that he would try to find us some injections and promised to come see us that very night. Late that night, after we had locked the house all up, we heard a motorcycle come in to our yard. It was Dr. Victor and a Mozambican friend of his. The friend was a Muslim. The man had the injections that he had brought up from South Africa, just to have for his own children in cases like this. But he offered them to us, free of charge. They were very expensive - he said they were $500.00. They are a series of five injections that must be given over a 28-day period. Even though the man was a Muslim, he said that he wanted to give them to us to show his appreciation for our coming to his country to help them. We were speechless. After we regained our composure, we asked the man if we could pray with him and thank God for this gift. We told him that the Bible says, "Every good and perfect gift comes from above." So we told him, that he might think that he was giving them to us, but that really, as a result of prayer, these injections were from God.

The Nigerian doctor came faithfully to our home over the next 28 days to give Timothy the five shots. Timothy was just terrified of shots. Several grown people would have to hold him down when it was shot time. We didn't know how the doctor was going to manage giving him these shots. So the first day, the doctor was trying to tell him how it didn't hurt and to be brave. Timothy was not buying the fact that it wasn't going to hurt. He begin to pitch such a fit, that the doctor decided that maybe if Timothy gave the doctor a shot, and he didn't cry, then that would help Timothy. So he rolled up his sleeve, and told Timothy how to give a shot, and allowed an eight-year-old boy to stick his arm! When he didn't cry or flinch, this gave Timothy the needed strength to go through the five injections!

God, again, proved to be our provider. His mercies never end - five free injections from a Muslim man, on the day of the dog bite, and a kind Nigerian Doctor who came to our house five times, and would never allow us to pay him.

Miracle #10- God Provided a Plane

One day, Mike was very ill with malaria. Due to some other symptoms that he had never had before when he had had malaria, we began to suspect he had another sickness on top of the medicine. He was very, very sick. In the back of our mind, we always knew that if things got very bad, that we could call our mission board and ask them to arrange a medical emergency evacuation - we could be picked up in our city, by a private plane with a doctor on board, and be flown to a nice hospital in South Africa. The main thing was to know when to call for this plane, and when not to. It costs about $35,000 for this to be arranged, so the mission board must know that it is an emergency! And with malaria, you never know how serious it is. You don't want to wait too late, because it can be fatal. Nor do you want to call the plane if it is really not necessary, because with malaria, you feel like you are going to die, but most of the time you recover! So you can't call them with every case!

In order for the mission board to arrange for this, they want to speak to a doctor or nurse in the city where you live. Many times they know the spouse or the parent of the sick patient may not be able to think clearly in a time of emergency. They need an unbiased medical opinion to know that this is truly an emergency. Because we did not have a doctor or nurse in our city at that time, we were on the phone back and forth with the mission board, trying to arrange the flight. Finally, after I assured them there was no doctor they could talk to, they agreed to talk to another missionary. Thus a missionary friend got on the phone and was able to assure the mission board, that this was indeed an emergency. We also didn't have a phone at the time, so all of this communication was very difficult in that we had to go down to the public phones and try to communicate with our mission board headquarters in Zimbabwe and our mission medical center in South Africa.

So plans were made for the plane to come the next day to take Mike to the hospital. This was the earliest they could come. Later on that day, another plane had already been summoned to come from South Africa to pick up another sick missionary with Operation Mobilization. We had a very dear family that lived next door to us from South Africa, Christopher and Jeanne. As our friend Christopher was helping to assess Mike's situation, he knew it was critical that Mike get to the hospital immediately. Christopher went to the home of the missionary in his organization that was ill, and as he saw her, he was able to see that she had turned the corner and was recovering. Miraculously, she had gotten better. So Christopher decided that it would be crucial for Mike to get on the earlier plane he had coming later on in the day, since the other missionary was better. So we called and canceled our medical evacuation plane, and Mike was put on the plane that was coming that very day!

Christopher and his family agreed to keep Timothy and Grace, and in a matter of 30 minutes, I had to pack for Mike and myself to leave for South Africa. I got on that plane, and felt such a great peace about leaving my children. Normally, that would have been quite difficult, because I wouldn't have had phone contact with them and we were going to another country. But, as I realized that God had provided this plane for Mike, I realized that He could surely take care of Timothy and Grace in our absence. The family that kept them had a radio, and they had a contact in South Africa whom we could call on the phone, and then they could patch it on to their radio. So we did try to talk to Timothy and Grace a few times, but they did not like the frustrations of trying to hear us on the radio- there was quite a delay and static. We would try to call, and they would say, "Hello", and then run away to play! I knew by that, that they were having the time of their lives - living with a family with five children!

As we got to the hospital, and realized that Mike had malaria, pneumonia and malaria- induced hepatitis, we knew it had been critical for him to come that very day. We marveled that God, in His providence had orchestrated all the circumstances, and had sent a plane to land in our town of Mocuba on the very day that he needed it. God healed the other missionary, and saw fit to provide for Mike. Due to the isolation and desolation of Mocuba, planes didn't land every day, not even every week, or month. We serve a wonderful God, who does abundantly more than we can ask or think.

Chapter 9

THE MIRACLE GOD DID NOT DO
- HAVING TO LEAVE MOZAMBIQUE

A FTER THIS medical evacuation to South Africa, our mission
board told us, that we had to leave Mozambique. This case
of malaria was Mike's 15th episode. The doctors told us
that if Mike got malaria, even one more time, it could be fatal.
They talked seriously to us about them not wanting to bury Mike
in Mozambique. But when we returned home to Mocuba and
considered all that had happened, we honestly didn't feel a peace
about leaving. We really prayed about it and felt that we should
stay. Many people did not understand our decision, but we just
felt that we couldn't leave the Mozambican people. We decided
to really ask the people in America to pray for us and for them to
plead with God to keep malaria away from Mike. For a solid year
after this concerted prayer effort, Mike did not get malaria. Then
came the fateful day when he got it again, the first time after his
medical evacuation - case number 16. He was so sure that it was
just a random case, and that he would not get it again. Then came
case number 17. Again, he just knew it was a random time and it
would not happen again. Then on Christmas morning, 2003, he
woke up with all the symptoms - case number 18. He looked at
me on that Christmas morning, and said, "Amy, I can't do this
anymore. This is it - we will have to leave." I must say that was
one of the saddest days of my life.

We went to Johannesburg that Christmas and we talked to
the leaders of our organization and they began to consider other

jobs that we could move to. We wanted to move to the south of Mozambique, or the north of South Africa, and continue to work with the Mozambicans (many had fled to South Africa during the war). But even in this part of South Africa, there is malaria, so our board would not allow us to move there. We had six choices of places to move: five in South Africa, and one in Lesotho. Again, we prayed about it, and we felt inclined to work with the Xhosa people in Cape Town. We also knew Cape Town was a big city, and would have good schools for Timothy and Grace. They had lived in such isolation, that we did want them to have good schools, especially as they entered into those critical high school years.

We went back to Mozambique and began to pack our things. We praise God that in those months of packing and leaving, Mike did not get malaria again. The pastors and churches really were sad about our leaving. Many of them didn't understand of course that we would have to leave because of malaria. It is such a normal part of life for them; they don't know life without malaria. But we knew that we had to do what we had to do, even if they didn't understand.

It was a blessing the way that one young man responded. Celestino was a very special person; he became like a member of our family. We worked very closely with him in the ministry. When we broke the news to him, he said that this would obviously have to be the will of God, and that therefore he could not say anything against it. That was such a comforting statement.

Several missionaries came to help us pack our things into the shipping container – the same container that had brought our things from America six years ago. Our friends arrived the very day we had to load our things, so they assumed that I would have most of the things in boxes by then, since they were just helping to pack the container. We had to load it on this particular day, because a Mozambican customs official was there at our house to oversee everything we packed in there. Each box had to be numbered and then he had a list as to what was in the boxes. Well, the four missionaries arrived to help us and when they walked in our house it looked like we had done nothing! Nothing was packed up in the kitchen, and the refrigerator and freezer still had food in them and were still plugged in. (As you know, when you pack and move a refrigerator and freezer, it needs to be completely dry –

and defrosting takes a while!) Although some things were packed up, they were amazed that we had not done more packing. But honestly, I was in denial and so did not want to leave. I absolutely couldn't bear to pack our things away. I will never forget the kindness of those four missionaries that sweetly packed our things and literally helped me get through that day. That day was overcast and it began to rain. The weather was a reflection of how I felt in my heart. I had already cried buckets of tears.

We had many tearful goodbyes with our four workers - three guards and the lady that helped in the house. We just felt so hopeless as to how they would make it financially, now that we were leaving. The prospect for another job was slim. We really felt like we were leaving family. After packing our container, we packed our car with all the things we would need for the following year in Xhosa language school- for the six day drive to our new location. We would not see our furniture and things again for another year. It was very hard for us to give our animals away. The other missionaries had a huge send off for us, and we were off. My heart literally broke as we drove out of our driveway for the last time, and bid our workers, other friends and animals goodbye.

Grace had a bird, a cockatiel, that we had brought back with us from a trip to South Africa. It is really illegal to bring live animals through borders, so we had smuggled the animal in months ago, and now we were having to take it back to South Africa. It was in the back seat with us, and when we got to the border, we had to hide it. We were praying it wouldn't begin to sing while the border guards were inspecting our car!

We moved to Grahamstown, South Africa and began Xhosa language school. We did not cope very well during that time as we grieved. It was so hard to understand why God did not answer our prayers for Him to protect Mike from malaria. I must admit, I was quite angry with God. It was hard to pray and hard to focus on the task ahead. We did finish language school after a year and moved to our new permanent assignment, Cape Town.

Although we were glad to be out of language school, and to get our furniture and possession agains, the anger and grief continued. After a few months in Cape Town, I went to a concert by Bill Drake, a Christian musician from America. He sang the song from the book of Job, Job 1:21 that says: "You give and take away, you give and take away, My heart will choose to say, Lord blessed be your name."

I felt the Lord speak to me in an audible voice, "I gave you 5 ½ years in Mozambique, and now I have taken that away, and you have not praised me." I heard it over and over again. I confessed my sin and asked God to forgive me for being angry with Him for not answering our prayers - to keep malaria away from Mike, so we could stay in Mozambique. I felt such a peace over my soul, like rivers flowing over all that pain. I must say, I did continue to grieve, but I could see hope for the future.

While we were in Grahamstown for that year, we never met anyone that spoke Portuguese. That had been such a huge part of our lives - thinking in and preparing messages in Portuguese. Now, we were trying to speak Xhosa, but down deep our love was for the beautiful Portuguese language. I thought in it, dreamed in it, and loved to read the Bible in Portuguese.

After we moved to Cape Town, we met many people who spoke Portuguese - there are 40,000 Angolan refugees in Cape Town, plus others from Brazil and refugees from Mozambique. There are two Portuguese Baptist churches, and we love to worship there and sing the beautiful songs. I was asked to teach English to Angolan refugees each Saturday and loved that ministry. We began to befriend and support the 3 Angolan Seminary students. Then we were asked to teach at the Portuguese Bible School that they had in town. I would do one module, and then Mike would do another. We got so close to the 14 students that we taught. They were at the end of their three-year course, and we were able to teach that last year. Now they have all graduated, and there are no other Angolans that are studying, so God provided that teaching time for us at the exact time that we were here! It is just so amazing to us, that while we were in language school, we never met anyone that spoke Portuguese, thus allowing us to be able to focus on Xhosa. But after moving to Cape Town, we were able to feel the Lord using us as we encountered the many refugees from Portuguese countries. We didn't want to feel that that skill of speaking Portuguese was in vain. Once you learn a language, you want to use it!

One of the ministries that I am involved in here in Cape Town is the Bible Way Correspondence Course. (This is the same ministry I did in Mozambique - mainly in the prisons). It is a series of ten books; each having an exam. After completing the ten exams, one gets a certificate for advanced Bible knowledge. The books are in many of the African languages here in South Africa - Zulu, Xhosa, Sotho, just to name a few. But I began to be burdened that they did not offer the books in Portuguese, since there are so many Portuguese speakers here in South Africa. So I called the Bible Way office and asked them why they did not offer the books in Portuguese. The lady on the phone told me that as far as she knew, they did not exist. She went on to tell me all about the war in Mozambique and how all the books were destroyed! She didn't know that I had been a missionary in Mozambique and that I personally had all the books myself! I told her, no, that I had lived in Mozambique and that I brought the ten books out and wanted to make them available to all the Angolans and Mozambicans living in South Africa. There was silence on the other end of the phone, and the lady began to cry. She just absolutely could not believe that they were available - she said they had looked for them for years! So now the course is available in Portuguese and we have already had 20 students graduate from the course. It is also available to the prisoners, and I have been corresponding with an Angolan prisoner here in the South African prison, and he is doing the course. This was one of those "God moments", when I just knew that He had engineered the circumstances. So often God reminds me that the years in Mozambique were not in vain - that God will still use our skills in Portuguese.

Chapter 10

WHEN GOD SAID "NO"

THROUGHOUT THE Word of God, He has promised to listen to our prayers and answer them. It says in Isaiah 65:24, that He will answer us even before we call. The only requirement is for us to call upon Him - after that, He promises to answer. We know that He answers, but that his answers can be "yes", "no" or "wait". It may not be the response we want.

I praise God for all the times He answered prayers throughout history. We have many incidences of this recorded in the Bible. Moses prayed for the children of Israel to find water, and God made water come out of a rock. Hannah prayed for a child, and God gave her Samuel. Elijah prayed for a miraculous manifestation of His glory to show His power to the people who were worshipping false gods. He sent fire from heaven and it burned up the altar. There are countless times in the Bible when God answered people's prayers, just as they asked.

We know also that there are times in the Bible when it says that our prayers are not even heard by God. We feel at times when we pray that our prayers are just hitting the ceiling and not going to the Father. Yet this really happens at times, when God does not hear. This is generally because we have sin in our heart or broken relationships with other people or with God. Other times the Bible says that He hears, but that He refuses to answer in the way that we want. This happens when our motives are impure, and when we lack faith.

All of us have wrestled with times in our lives when we didn't understand why God didn't answer a prayer like we wished. We have all had times when we prayed earnestly for God to heal someone, and they died. Where is God in these times? We all ask if there was something else we could have done. If we would have prayed more, prayed longer, prayed with more faith, would our friend have been healed?

I am sure our heroes in the Bible wrestled with this as well. Moses prayed to be able to enter the Promised Land and God said "no". King David prayed and fasted for a week for his son not to die, but he died. Paul prayed three times for the Lord to take away His thorn in the flesh. God didn't. The Psalmist felt this so intently when he said, " I am worn out from calling for help; my throat is parched. My eyes fail, looking for my God" (Psalm 69:3, 119:82).

We also know from God's Word that "his ways are higher than our ways, and his thoughts than our thoughts." We must believe that if He says "yes", "no" or "wait", He has a higher and greater purpose in mind. He has the big picture and we see one small frame at a time.

This is a book of how God answered our prayers. Chapter Eight tells about ten miraculous miracles that happened in Mozambique. This was when God said "yes" to our plea. Yet this is also the story of how God did not answer the desire of our heart. After my husband, Mike, had 18 cases of malaria, we knew that we would not be able to stay in Mozambique. We had prayed and had asked hundreds of other Christians to pray for God to protect Mike from malaria – literally, people were praying for him all over the globe. We kept trusting that God would answer our prayer. Mike was healthy for one year after he had case number 15. We praised God for answered prayer. We felt so happy to know that hundreds had joined us in this prayer support. But then Mike got cases number 16, then 17, and then 18. After a year of health, the cases began to come very frequently. Obviously, God had chosen in His providence to not protect Mike from malaria. We knew this meant that we would have to leave the country.

So then how did we feel? We went through the gamut of emotions and thoughts. We blamed ourselves for sin and for lack of faith. Then we blamed others for not praying for us. When we began to accept that this must be the will of God for us, but then why? When Mike got case number 15, the doctors said if he keeps getting it, he would die. How could we leave our friends, our workers, and the other missionaries? How could we uproot our children who were very content? How could we adapt to a new country and learn a new language, and completely new culture? Was He protecting us from harm that only He could see in the future? How could He want us to leave there, after we had learned the language, and built relationships with the nationals? We were just beginning to enter a Muslim area on the coast. Was it spiritual warfare? I must say after looking back on it all, I don't have many answers. But I do know He is a good God and I must trust Him. There is a beautiful song that says, "When you don't see His hand, trust His heart." We really didn't see His hand in it all. So we quickly had to pick another assignment, pack our belongings and leave.

I must say that six years later, there is still not a missionary in this area. We wonder daily about all the churches and pastors we worked with. How are they all coping? Who is taking care of the physical needs for medicine and other help for all those people that came daily to our gate? All we can do it trust in our Heavenly Father. And I don't mean that lightly, or glibbly. It is a trust that causes us to surrender our very lives and that of our children.

Chapter 11

IT'S ALWAYS IMPORTANT
TO KEEP YOUR HUMOR

I N STRESSFUL times, we know it is always important to try to find the humorous side of life. There always is one, but we don't always see it. It makes life much more bearable. Immediately, when we moved to Mozambique, we tried to keep our sense of humor. The first thing that shocked us was the amount of things a lady can carry on her head! We saw ladies daily carrying full buckets of water, or a coconut, or her clothes or dishes she needed to wash in the river. But the funniest thing we saw was a lady carrying a huge watermelon on her head!

To be an African, you have to be able to carry any load. A mother would many times have a baby on her back, another child in her arms, and then a load on her head. It would be normal to see a little girl of four years old, with her little sister on her back-hardly able to walk! The men would need to be able to carry their family on the family bike. During our time there, we tried to see who won the record of carrying the most people on their bike. We often saw a man riding his bike, and then his wife on the back and then several children on the center bar, with several chickens tied upside down on the handle bars. Even one-legged people could ride bikes! One day we even saw a bike with 20 cases of cokes stacked on it – with 24 glass bottles in each case.

It was also fun to see how much those mini-vans/taxis could carry If they held 15 people legally, there would be 30 people inside, with all their suitcases tied to the top. Sometimes several goats would be tied on the top too. And they were so good at tying things, so that rarely did anything fall off. There would always be ducks and chickens, even pigs tied to the top.

I also had to keep my humor when we went to church. Our church was just a mud hut in the midst of many houses. It had very little yard around the church. All property is public property. We had no educational space, so we taught Sunday School outside under a tree. One of the neighbors that lived beside the church raised ducks. They are the loudest creatures God ever made. I would be trying to teach, and they would start quacking and squalking. Then many times they came right into the circle of chairs where I was teaching and they mated. It is hard to carrying on teaching the Bible with mating ducks in the middle of the classroom!

Essential Business

One of the main subjects that can be humorous, revolve around the bathroom (toilet). In Mozambique, very few houses had plumbing, so it is normal to use an outhouse. Generally, they will have one place in which you do your minor functions (number 1), and another place to do the major functions (number 2). The first place would just be a square enclosure with four walls made of bamboo. The second place would be a latrine that was either under ground or above ground. But to have a latrine, means you are better off than the person that just has the grass enclosure. So if you have a latrine, you have to keep it locked, so that it doesn't get filled up with all your neighbors visiting it! (Keep in mind, that in Africa, you live in community - hardly anything can be called yours - it has to be shared.) So the church had a nice in-ground latrine, and therefore had to keep it locked. So, if you needed the toilet in the middle of the four-hour church service, you would have to go up to the leader/pastor on stage and ask for the key! So everyone knew what you were fixing to do!! I would almost rather die than have to go to the front of the church and ask for the key! There was never toilet paper either, so that was a standard that you would have to bring in your purse - at all times!

Because there were separate buildings for separate functions, when you first visited a church or house, they would show you where the "toilets" were. When I would go to churches for women's meetings where I would be camping out for the weekend, they would show me the place to do the minor functions, and the place to do the major functions. You would also take a bath in the enclosure that you would urinate in. They would bring you a bucket of hot water that they had warmed over the stove, and you would sponge bathe. So you can imagine how important it was to have some waterproof shoes - as the shower location was used for other purposes!

One time, Mike took several pastors to Malawi to an evangelism meeting. This was the first time that they had been introduced to a flush toilet. Mike was explaining to them that they must go to the toilet in their dorm room, and not outside. He showed them how to sit or stand, and then how to flush it. This flushing motion just boggled their mind! Their main question was, "Where does it go?" For it to just disappear was beyond them! For years, they have had to carry shovels to bury their business, and for it to disappear was just too good to be true!

At this same meeting, they were given money for food, and then taken to the grocery shop to buy their food. They decided to just buy one loaf of bread and split it between them, and then just pocket the other money to take home to their families. They all gathered together in the shop, around this one loaf of bread, and they were trying to figure out how much it cost, because of course, they were in a different country with a different currency. So they were having to figure out the exchange rate, and to see how much money each of them must give. The security threw them out, thinking they were trying to steal things or that they were planning a burglary!

Food

The second main thing that missionaries laugh about is national food. When we were at our house, we could control what we ate, and many times just ate normal American food. But when we were camping out at the churches for our different meetings and services, we would have to eat what they gave us. One night, they gave me pumpkin leaves in a sauce on top of the corn meal mush. I took one bite and thought I would just die. Normally I could eat most things, but this was too much. So it was about dusk when they gave me my plate. They normally just sit around and watch you eat, because everything a white person does is entertainment to them. So they would watch how I would eat and what I would eat. So after that first bite, I knew I wasn't going to be able to eat it. So I had to stall and stall, and make conversation, waiting for the sun to go down. After it went down, it was pitch black and they wouldn't be able to watch me eat, nor be offended that I didn't eat. So in the dark, I just quickly threw my food in a little bag that I had with me, and then threw it away when I got home! I know that sounds terrible, but I had no other choice - because I would have offended them had I not eaten it. For cases like this, one would always bring food from home. So after a meal like they gave me, I would then go in my tent and eat my crackers and peanut butter, or M&M's, or Snickers. Since I hated camping out, I would save my most favorite American snack for times like this to reward myself!

The other worst thing I did (this is a time of confession), was during a Lord's Supper observance. Usually, the church would ask Mike to prepare the juice and the bread for the Lord's Supper. So he would mix up the red Kool-aid and bring the bread. But this time, the Mozambican pastor brought some red juice he had made and the bread. Since you cannot drink the water in Mozambique, and if you did, you would be deathly ill. I knew if I took that one little drink of communion, I would be sick. So I was sitting near a window. As they prayed to thank the Lord for the wine, I chuncked the juice out the window! The funny thing is that our church was in a community of houses - with people all around. While we were in church, the neighbors that weren't Christians would be at home playing their loud music, or washing clothes. So I am sure the neighbors wondered why all of a sudden someone poured some juice out of the church window! I told the Lord I was so sorry, and hope He has forgiven me!

Timothy is a very picky eater. One weekend, he went to camp out with Mike in the bush while Mike was doing a church visit and revival services. They kept fixing Timothy a plate of their corn meal mush and gravy and chicken. Timothy just couldn't find it in his heart to eat it. And it is a huge insult to refuse their food. I had luckily sent Timothy with a loaf of pumpkin bread to eat in case of emergency. It got quite embarrassing for Mike to explain to the group, that Timothy wouldn't eat their food. So finally, Mike told them that Timothy only eats "food his mother fixes" (*comida da mãe*). That seemed to satisfy them, and Timothy survived the weekend!

Chicken Stories

Here are some of the 'chicken stories' we had-

1.   Mike was given a chicken as a gift as he left a church after having been with them for the weekend. They tied the chicken's feet together and put him in the back of Mike's truck, along with many bananas and sweet potatoes and other gifts. Mike's tent and water and other things were also in the back of the truck. Many times when Mike would arrive home late on a Sunday night, he would not unpack his truck, as he was too tired from the journey. (He didn't know there was a chicken in there!) So on Monday morning, Mike found the chicken and it had laid an egg - with its legs tied together. Pretty talented chicken!

2.   We would go to the local restaurant for a break sometimes. But if you wanted to go, you would need to place your order the day before, or if you placed it that day, it would take three hours to prepare your meal. They first had to catch the chicken, and then build the fire, etc. One time we were at the restaurant, and it was taking very long for them to bring us our meal. They brought three plates of chicken and French fries, and then they brought me the last plate. As I bit into my chicken, I realized that it was not chicken. Although the meat was not burnt, it was very dark and tough. Then as I took a second bite, I found a bee bee in my chicken! When I asked them about it, they admitted that one of their chickens had flown away, and they didn't have another. They had had to go and hunt a guinea fowl, and then kill it and cook it for me! They had made that substitution without asking me.

3.   When we left to go on our first furlough back to America, we were given three chickens for us to take with us to eat on the road! That was normal for them; when they travel, there are no fast food restaurants or shops along the way - they take everything with them. So they were being very kind to give us three chickens to eat on our way to America. I can just see us trying to get into the airplane with a live chicken!

4.   When we were on vacation with my parents at the famous Island of Mozambique, we were eating right on the beach at a lovely restaurant. On the menu was steak and many delicious things that they were 'out' of that day. So we ordered a plate of chicken. When it came, there was absolutely no meat on this chicken. (We were used to there being very little meat on the chickens, and it being very tough - but this had hardly any meat on it). We laughed and laughed about this chicken - that it didn't even squawk when they went to kill it - it just laid down and said, "Please kill me; I don't have enough meat on my bones to keep running around!"

Clothing

The Mozambican ladies would generally wear wrap-around skirts of African print that they had bought, with T-shirts that came from either America or Europe. The men would wear jeans or pants with these same used T-shirts. These T-shirts and other clothes arrived in Mozambique in huge shipping containers. They were meant to be given away for free, but the government would sell all the clothes to middlemen that would then sell them to the people in a used clothing market. So many times the Mozambicans would wear T-shirts with English slogans which they had no idea what it said. One day a *man* was taking up the offering in the Baptist church with a shirt that said, "I'd rather be 40 than pregnant". We about cracked up when we saw that! Another time a man took up the offering in a Budweiser beer shirt - he had no idea what a Budweiser was! One day as we sat in an un-air-conditioned church, when the weather was about 100 degrees outside, a man had a shirt on that said, "Is it hot in here, or it is just me?"! Another day, a lady in the choir had a shirt on that said, "No funk, No Glory". The shirts would advertise sporting teams, colleges, restaurants, etc. in the states. Men would wear McDonalds uniforms, and of course, they had no idea what they were wearing. Little boys would wear Barbie shirts, and never know the difference.

Language Woes

Communication is always a very difficult thing when you are speaking a foreign language. We have made our share of mistakes!

One night, we had a family over for supper at our house. I was quite nervous, as they were our first visitors. The mother of the family offered to help, and I told her she could pour the drinks. I told her that I had Coke, water, and several types of juice, and they could choose. Well, she didn't understand the "choose" part, and she mixed all the drinks together! She started with a little Coke, and then added a little water, and then poured a small amount of all the different juices in the cup. She kept shaking her head, as though she knew this was crazy, but I didn't know how to tell her in Portuguese that this was not what I wanted! I am sure she wondered about these crazy white people. Every time anyone would take a sip, they would wince and try not to complain about this horrible drink I was giving them!

Easter Egg Hunts

Because Tim and Grace were small, we would try to celebrate all the normal American traditions. So each Easter, we would have an egg hunt. The first year, we went to the market and bought about 3 dozen eggs, dyed them and had an egg hunt. Our house worker kept asking me the purpose of this. After we dyed them and hid them, we normally wouldn't eat them. Since most Mozambicans are generally hungry most of the time, and never have enough to eat, this was beyond her. She just couldn't believe that we weren't going to eat them after we had boiled them and dyed them. I was so ashamed of myself after that day, realizing how wasteful I was! After that, I would put a hole in the end of the egg, and blow the contents out before dying them and hiding them, so as not to waste the eggs!

The next year, I got my Mom to send plastic eggs, so it wouldn't be a bad witness to the nationals that we were so wasteful (even though I did blow them out but they didn't know that). So we had all the kids stay in the house, while the adults hid the plastic eggs full of candy. We had a small fence that surrounded our house, and everything we did was watched by many eyes. So they stared in fascination as we hid these brightly colored plastic eggs in the bushes! So when the adults left to go inside to call the children, the local children jumped the fence and starting taking all the eggs! Needless to say, we didn't have an egg hunt that year, as they were all stolen before we had a chance to get outside!

What Does a Missionary
Take to Church in Her Purse?

As I have mentioned, our church services were normally four hours long. Since Mike was generally out of town visiting one of the other 100 churches in our region, the kids and I would go to church on our bikes. I would have to pack quite a bit to go to church - here is a list of what would be in my bag:

*The Bible in 2 languages (English and Portuguese) - so I could always be ready when called on to participate

*The Portuguese hymnbook (no hymnbooks are left in the pews - each person has to buy their own; thus many aren't fortunate to have them)

*Toilet paper

*Enough cold water and snacks for the children to last during the hot four hours

*A little hand-held fan

*Things for the kids to do: crayons, coloring books, toys

*Money for the offering

*My maraca and tambourine

*My notes for teaching Sunday School to the youth

*And, generally, I would have some medicine or something that a member in the church had asked me to bring the previous Sunday

You had to always be prepared!

My Parents' Experience

It was a blessing when we had visitors to come to see us. In 1999, my parents came to visit, and this was such a highlight for us. I must say, first of all, that my parents were immediately greatly honored and revered because of their age. Very few people in Mozambique live past 40, and thus very few people have gray hair. So, if you have gray hair, you are greatly respected. They kept asking how old they were! They were still in their 60's, and we would tell them that Mike's grandparents were still alive in their 80's, and they really thought we were lying!

They wanted to experience everything possible during their stay. One Sunday we all went to a church out in the bush. We drove an hour and a half to get there by car. At one point, we had to cross a river on a bridge that looked very suspect! There are no bridge inspectors in Mozambique, and it is a wonder more don't fall in. My mother refused to drive across the bridge in the car - just knowing there was no way that bridge would hold up our big truck! So she got out and walked across the bridge! Praise the Lord; again, it didn't fall in. Then we had to walk an hour and a half once we got off the road. All the while that you are walking in Mozambique, and you ask a Mozambican how far it is to your destination, they always answer, "it is very close" (*muito perto*). It could be five hours away, but they would always say, "*Muito perto*"! We began to realize that that meant nothing. They were just trying to appease you! During the one and a half hour walk, they came to a small river they had to cross. They generally had a canoe for Mike to ride when he had been there before, but it wasn't available this time. So Mike was trying to tell the Mozambicans that his in-laws were old and they couldn't cross the river without the canoe. So a little Mozambican man that was about 5 feet tall and weighed 80 pounds, told Mike that he was going to carry my mom across! He goes to try to pick her up, and my mom just hiked up her skirt and walked across herself! As a gift for our visit, we were given a chicken, and Tim carried that chicken the whole way back. So we drove three hours and walked another three that day!

Mike and my mother crossing the river to get to church.

Timothy carrying the chicken for an hour and a half
that we received as a gift after the church visit.

Being Prepared for Anything

One of the worst things about being in the long African church service is that they are very flexible, and can put you on the spot in a minute. They could call you up to preach, and you would have no idea that they were going to! They could ask you to come and sing a song, or give a testimony and you just had to be ready. Well, one day, the church choir was singing a song they had made up on the Ten Commandments. They did kind of a recitation or rap, quoting each commandment, and then singing a little chorus in between each one. Well, we were sitting there enjoying this wonderful, creative, made-up song, and in the course of the song, when they were on Commandment number three, in rhythm, they said, "Now the missionaries will tell us Commandment number four"! And they wanted us to say it in a foreign language in rhythm, with no advance warning! We just had to say, "We don't know!" And afterwards they came to us and said, "What kind of missionaries have been sent to us that don't even know the Ten Commandments?!"

Chapter 12

HARDSHIPS OF LIFE IN MOZAMBIQUE

Leaving Family

ALTHOUGH THE blessings were very great, so were the hardships of life in Mozambique. I think every missionary would say that leaving family is probably the hardest thing of all. This was definitely true for me. I literally felt my heart was going to break when I said goodbye to my family at the airport. And I kept thinking that with each furlough and leaving again, that it would get easier. Only people that have done this can truly know the pain. And having a particularly close relationship with your family hurts more. I almost envy those missionaries that don't have close relationships, and really don't have a hard time leaving their families. I have said it before, but I know that it has not only been a sacrifice for me, but for my family and for Mike's family as well. Sometimes I have felt the price was too high, and the sacrifice too great. God's grace is sufficient, but I must say, I have cried myself to sleep many nights in these past ten years due to the separation from family. Holidays are the worst. The mission family is great, and we do celebrate many holidays together. But nothing can take the place of those natural family relationships.

The writings of Jim and Elisabeth Elliott (former missionaries to Ecuador) have particularly been meaningful to me. In a letter to his mother about this same topic, he wrote, "Remember that we have bargained with him who bore a Cross, and in His ministry to those disciples His emphasis was upon sacrifice, not of worldly goods, so much as upon family ties." I feel I have really sacrificed none if you consider worldly goods or material possessions that I would have had if I weren't a missionary, but I do feel the pain of the great sacrifice of family ties.

Malaria

The second greatest hardship was the exposure to malaria. Again, only someone that has lived in a malarial setting can understand this! It absolutely consumes one's thinking! One is always aware to not go outside from dusk to dawn, and it is not easy to always be locked up inside from 6 p.m. to 6 a.m. One is always worried about having the proper medicine - both the daily prophylactics, and the medicine needed when you actually get malaria. Many of these medicines could not be gotten in Mozambique, so one would have to plan ahead to have the necessary supply. And when one got sick, one had to think about how you would get a blood test, and who would read the slide. In the five and a half years, we had times when there were no doctors available, and other times when we would need to go to Malawi (a 6-hour trip on a dirt road) to see a doctor. Each time one of my family got malaria, I was constantly worried that it could turn into cerebral malaria and be fatal - there was always that possibility in the back of my mind.

Since we had such a nice missionary community in Mozambique, it seemed sometimes, during the peak summer months (which was the mosquito breeding time), I was always nursing someone with malaria. Many of them were single missionaries and I would make soup for them, or take them food. The topic of conversation seemed to always be "who had malaria this week". Sometimes, it was the only topic, as so many were sick. Sometimes I got tired of thinking about it.

One realizes the pressure one was under only when one leaves the situation and looks back at it. When we would travel to South Africa for an annual vacation, since it is not a malarial area, the freedom we felt was amazing! We could stay outside in our yard past dusk, sitting outside having a barbeque with friends. We were not constantly checking the house for mosquitoes, or worrying if we got bitten, because the mosquitoes there don't carry malaria.

The thing that made the malaria in Mozambique worse was the fact that Mike's job caused him to have to cover a huge geographical region. We were the only Baptist missionaries in the Lomwe tribal area, so it was common for him to have to drive eight hours, one way, to a church. Malaria was such a problem, because it would take him all day to drive somewhere, and then after the meetings and revivals, it would be impossible to drive back the same day. So it always entailed sleeping at the churches in a tent. He would try to wear repellent and socks (mosquitoes like ankles), and would try to get inside his tent at dark, but it is impossible to be in your tent from six p.m. to six a.m. while the nationals are so happy that you are there and they want a service - sometimes lasting all night!

Many people may wonder what it feels like to have malaria. You generally begin to have a terrible headache, unlike other headaches. Then you begin to have a high fever, and it spikes, and then subsides. You also have terrible chills and joint and body aches, like the flu. You also can have nausea and vomiting and diarrhea. At times, you can begin to hallucinate and are delirious. It can cause anemia and damage to your liver. The worst symptoms usually go away in four to five days if you take the medicine, but you feel very weak and generally washed out for two weeks. The problem comes when you take one medicine and it doesn't work. Malaria in many parts of Mozambique has become resistant to some types of medicine. So if you take one medicine and it doesn't work, than you have to take another kind. Left untreated, it is almost always fatal. Then there is the cerebral type that causes seizures and, many times, death. These types of malaria call for injections of quinine. Malaria kills many people each year in Africa, and is the number two killer after AIDS. Many missionaries struggle with malaria, as we don't have any immunities built against it. We do know missionaries from other organizations that have lost children to malaria.

During these 5 ½ years, Mike had malaria 18 times, Grace five times and Timothy, five. So 28 times, I nursed sick family members and worried if and when they would recover. It was a very heavy burden. I guess the Lord knew I couldn't get malaria, because I was too busy caring for everyone else!

Many people have asked why Mike got malaria so many times and I didn't get it. Well, first of all, I got to stay home with the children while Mike was in the bush in his tent three nights a week. The second reason is that some people are just susceptible to being bitten. Even in America or here in South Africa where there is no malaria, we can be at an outdoor barbeque, and Mike will comment about how he is getting eaten by the mosquitoes. I will not even feel them or see them. So it is thought that some people attract mosquitoes and others don't.

Other people have asked why Mike did not take the necessary prophylactics medicine. Mike did try taking them and he did use mosquito repellent creams. But taking a prophylactic doesn't give 100% protection. It does help the case not be so severe. He did have disturbing side effects with each of the prophylactics and would stop taking one, and then take another kind. There was one medicine that he took once a week, and for three days after taking the pill, he would be so sick. So, eventually he had tried them all and they all had unpleasant side effects. Also, people that come into a malarial area for a week or two don't mind the side effects. But if you live in a malarial country year in and year out, you don't want to constantly feel bad because of the side effects. So Mike was just unfortunately very susceptible to mosquito bites. I am sure Mike could have been more diligent in trying to prevent the mosquitoes from biting him - using more creams, and sprays. But again, when you live there year in and year out, it is easy to let your guard down because you can't be so vigilant day after day.

Language

Language was also another hardship. We tried so hard to learn Portuguese, and we did quite well. We could function and make ourselves understood. But Portuguese will always be seen as the "white man's colonial language". So every Mozambican had their tribal dialect that they also spoke. And many times in the rural areas, and even in the cities, the women and older people could not speak much Portuguese. This is because during the many years of war, the women were not allowed to go to school. So we were so proud that we had learned this foreign language, but we could only communicate with a percentage of the population! If we would have stayed in Mozambique, we would have needed to study and master the local dialect, Lomwe, next.

Heat

One cannot underestimate the difficulty that came from the soaring temperatures. It would be over 100 degrees for sometimes weeks on end, and even get to be 110-120. It would actually start affecting you physically - in that you were hot from the minute you woke up, until you went to sleep! We did have AC window units in our bedrooms, but the electricity was so weak that there was not enough voltage to run all three of them. And then there were the nights that we had no power, and without a fan or AC, the heat, even at night, made it very difficult to sleep. I remember several nights just sleeping on the bare concrete floor, since concrete is usually cooler! The best part of the day would be a drive in the car to the market - with the AC running full blast!

I think the hottest day of the year was Christmas Day. I can remember standing in my kitchen trying to cook a Christmas dinner and sweat just pouring off my face and down my back. So to cheer myself up, I would try to play Christmas music. But with so many songs about snow and the cold, it was hard to relate. Then I think each CD I have has the song on there, "I'll Be Home for Christmas", and I would run as fast as I could to shut that song up! I can hardly bear to hear it, even now! Christmas in the hot time of the year means you can't wear Christmas sweaters. I would want to dress little Grace in her cute Christmas clothes, but when it is 110 outside, it just doesn't work! Being hot on Christmas is bad enough, but doesn't compare at all to being away from family. But God had his way of reassuring us. One year on Christmas day, we looked up in the sky, and we saw the biggest, brightest double rainbow! It was sent just for me!

Our first Christmas was in language school. The temperature was over 100 and we were miserable, not only with the heat, but with being away from family. We had an AC unit in the living room of our language school house, but it didn't work. But on Christmas Day, we decided to try it one more time - and, can you believe, God gave us a wonderful Christmas present - the AC worked for that one day, and that one day only!

It is hard to describe the heat. But one day, we looked up and we saw all these brown spots appearing on our walls. It was like someone was flinging brown paint on our walls. We were so puzzled as to what it was. But we finally realized that there was so much humidity in the air that the rust on the ceiling fans had turned to liquid. And each time it went around, it was spewing the brown rust on the walls! Now, that is a hot day!

Lack of Medical Care

Also, the lack of medical care was huge. I am sure this has come through strongly as you have read this book. From the times we needed stitches, to broken bones, to malaria, to parasites - just the fact that we lacked medical care really affected us. We had to trust in the Lord so much that He would provide the medicine/treatment we needed for every ailment! God did provide in miraculous ways - praise His holy name. It was such a blessing to have to pray about *everything*- to find the medicine, or to find a person to give an injection, for example.

Throughout this book, at times you will read that we did have a doctor in town.   These doctors were generally on contracts with the government and they would agree to serve for a year at a time. Then, due to the workload and poor conditions, these doctors would not renew their contracts. So in the 5 ½ years we were there, we did have a doctor available for about half of that time. But there was still the lack of available medicines, hospitals and facilities.

One time, I was bitten by a poisonous spider. A huge area on my leg was affected, and it was getting infected. I went to the hospital in Malawi, and they admitted me immediately, saying I must be operated on that very day. They had to cut a very deep hole in my leg to get all the infection out, because I had waited too long to get to the hospital. For the wound to heal, it had to heal from the inside out - they couldn't stitch it. So each day, Mike would have to put a solution inside the wound. It smelled and burned like alcohol on a wound. It was very traumatic, and for weeks I wondered if the wound would ever close up! Since you would have to drive 7 hours to the hospital, you couldn't go back in a few days or even a week for follow-up. So, many times we were left to wonder how things were going to turn out!

Vast Job Responsibilities

The churches were being planted so quickly, mostly by the Mozambican pastors and leaders, that it was hard to keep up with them all. It is what has been termed a "church planting movement." We would just get word that another one had been started in this village, and they would want Mike to come to train them in how to be a church. There were about 100 of these churches that Mike would need to visit. If he went out and saw maybe three a week, you can see how long it would be to visit all these church plants. With just 52 weeks in a year, it was therefore not possible to even visit one time per year! So the job load was very hectic. On top of this leadership training and Biblical training (none of these leaders would get to go to a Seminary - Mike was the seminary!), he had the agricultural part to his job too. Every church expected Mike to come in and really help them with their gardens (they had to raise all their own food). The expectations were great, because they all wanted free seeds and hoes, etc. It was easy to feel discouraged, because we knew we were letting some of the people down that had unrealistic expectations of us.

Nationals' Attitudes

I think all missionaries would say that there is a hardship in that many times the nationals don't know why you have come to their country to be a missionary. Our white faces, usually to them, means money. In colonialism, the whites lorded over the Africans and lived very comfortably, while the nationals struggled. And still to this day, they see white faces that come in as aid workers, or UN officials, and they always come to quickly do a project, such as digging a well, and then they leave. They don't usually build relationships. So the Africans were used to seeing white people and feeling like their only job was to finance what they wanted to do. I could write another book on this alone!

When we moved to Mocuba, the church was a mud hut with a thatched roof. They immediately thought the reason we came was to finance the building of their church building. So in front of the whole church at a business meeting, they said how happy they were that we were going to finance the whole project. When we replied that we would be happy to "help" and "do our part", that meant to them that we were accepting their proposal. When the pastor and leader came over one day to get all the money, we were shocked! We told them that we didn't have that kind of money- it equaled thousands of dollars. Again, they didn't understand that we would "help"- to them that meant pay for the whole thing. We had many very difficult business meetings where the local leadership put us on the spot, and then called us liars when we didn't come through with all the money. And because Mike had to travel so much, I was at these business meetings many times by myself and felt very vulnerable and even taken advantage of. Then you have the language difficulties and I would have to answer in front of the church in Portuguese, and if I didn't say things correctly, they could get the completely wrong idea. I must say that I had to apply the verses in the Bible that says we must forgive people not seven times, but seventy times seven. During the course of the 5 ½ years there were many things that they said to us that were offensive. We didn't have the option of getting angry and leaving – we had to make it work.

Not only does the local church not know why we had come, but also the national Baptist Convention. Each year when we would go to this meeting, the elected leaders would also make it clear that us missionaries where not doing enough! They also had expectations, i.e., for us to build seminaries and more church buildings, etc. One year they made a plan for how missionaries and the nationals could work together. It was a ten point plan, that included:

*We had to let them know wherever we went - for instance; we had to get their permission to go on furlough, or to go on vacation, etc.

*Soon, all the cars and houses of the missionaries would have to be put in their names and given to the leaders of the Baptist Convention

It was quite painful at the time to again realize that they did not understand why we had come - to evangelize, train the Pastors, show the *JESUS* film, do agricultural work, etc. We knew we were putting in so many hours and giving of our lives, but some seemed to not appreciate the things we had been sent to do by the IMB.

Problems in the Churches

Because the churches were starting so quickly, at times the people were not discipled properly, and they would bring in the ancestral worship and combine it with their Christianity. Because many of the churches didn't have a trained pastor, at times, anything would be allowed. In our area, there were only seven pastors that had been through either Seminary or the equivalent training by Mike and the other missionary, John, who was two hours away. So you can see how many churches had leaders that had little or no training.

In our local Mocuba church, the pastor was a trained nurse and many Sundays had to work. He was so busy, that many times, he didn't come to church, and then he would not line up anybody to preach, or teach the adult Sunday School class. As much as we tried to talk with him, he never changed, and the people didn't seem to mind. We would get there, and they would expect us to speak and that really wasn't fair to not be asked ahead of time. Polygamy and drinking were such problems and it was always heartbreaking when a leader in the church would start drinking heavily and fall away, or take another wife. It seemed we were always dealing with a problem in one of the churches.

We were very close to a man named Saca. He was the leader of the Mocuba church. For three years while we were there, our pastor was in medical school in the capital city - far from our town. So Saca filled in for him. He was not a trained pastor/leader, but seemed to love the Lord and kept things organized while the pastor was away. He had a good job, had a motorcycle and really was a fine man. The last year that we were there, he started drinking heavily. It would be heartbreaking to see him drunk downtown, or staggering down the streets. His wife was so embarrassed, and it was so sad for his five daughters. I always wonder what happened to him.

I was also very close to a women named Angela. She was the president of the WMU- the Women's Missionary Union. She was very dedicated and I also trained her in teaching Sunday School. She was a single mom to a teenage boy and two small children under five. One day, we noticed that she wasn't in church. This was very unlike her, as she was always there. When I went to her house to check on her, I found her teenage son with his two siblings. When I asked about his mom, he said that she had "gotten married", and moved to another city. The new "husband", a fairly wealthy man in Mozambican terms, didn't want kids around, as he had his own kids. So she just left the 15 year old son alone in his hut to care for his two siblings. Many times they had nothing to eat. Supposedly, she was going to send them food from time to time, but it rarely came. Later, she moved with her new husband back to our city, but she lived in a nice concrete house across town, and still neglected her three children. When that teenage boy would come to my Sunday School class, my heart would break. He was now expected to go to school, and raise his two siblings. I went to Angela and asked her how she could do this, and she told me that a good opportunity had come around for her to better herself, and she just did it. I can't judge her; I haven't walked in her shoes. But it seemed to me to be such a tragedy.

I was teaching the youth Sunday School class and had such a good group of young people. Many were older teenage boys. I was always so excited that they were coming, since many drop out of church by that time. I never heard or saw them with girlfriends, so I just assumed they were single. One day I was visiting in the home of one of them. I knew everyone in the home, but there was one young lady/girl I didn't know. I asked who she was. They told me that she was the 'wife' of the young teenage boy in my class! I began to ask about this, and realized that the culture was for a 16-17 year old boy to take "a wife" and start living with her in his parent's house. If they could have children together, then she was a good woman and would be kept. If she was infertile, he could get another "wife" (they always assumed infertility was the woman's fault, and wouldn't consider otherwise).

To get married legally by the state required a tremendous amount of money, which most didn't have. So we encouraged them to have a church wedding and give their relationship to the Lord, even if they couldn't afford to get married by the court. We had a few church weddings, and it was a blessing. The couple would bring their children along to the wedding, as most had had children already. (I will always be indebted to the ladies at Ephesus Baptist Church for making and sending us many beautiful wedding dresses, veils and even bouquets. So when they made the excuse that they couldn't afford a dress, I said that can't be an excuse!)

The mother of this young man was very close to me. Her name was Fatima. I was teaching her how to read weekly in our literary classes. Mike helped her with her garden. She enjoyed visiting us and loved when I would show her the large teaching pictures for children's Sunday School, as she had never seen anything like that - she had always just had to envision what the ark looked like, for example. The First Baptist Church of Mocuba started through a home Bible study that met in her house. She was the charter member. But one day, I was discussing the whole sex before marriage theme. She told me that was just my opinion, that "the Bible is just the white man's book." That absolutely broke my heart. Here was a leader in the church, and she really didn't feel the Bible was hers. Of course, if one doesn't believe the Bible pertains to them, they won't feel that the teachings are for them to obey. As we traveled and lived there longer, I heard this several other times, so it was the feeling of many.

One young man was very active in the church and he went with me weekly to the prison. He had a beautiful voice and knew the Bible so well. He also would travel with Mike to train the youth in other cities. One day, someone in the church told me that he had a 'wife' and two kids, and that since he knew it was wrong, he made her live at her parent's home in the rural area, far from our town. Because we were quite close to him, I asked him about it. He denied it! Again, that was the talk of the church that Raul had a 'wife.' We asked him again, and he finally admitted that they had been together for years now, but since he knew it was wrong, he made her live in the bush! So we went and met her, and led her to the Lord and encouraged them to have a church wedding. I got a dress for her, a veil, flowers and made them a cake. She then got to move to the city and live with him, and they were a fine young couple in the church.

Raul had absolutely no way to provide for his family. He walked with one crutch to compensate for a deformed leg. I taught him how to make potholders using coke and beer bottle caps. He would sew a small piece of cloth around the cap, and then join many of them together to form a potholder. He would ride his bike and collect the caps from the floors of bars and restaurants and worked very hard to sew them. I was able to sell these for him at various missionary meetings and to American friends. This gave him a very small income, but every bit helped.

I know many missionaries have made mistakes by forcing western culture on the nationals and expecting them to do things just like we do them, even when our traditions mean nothing to them. For instance, the white wedding dress. So we weren't trying to make them all have a traditional western wedding, but we were trying to get them to own up to what they were doing! They needed the church to bless it, and if they already had kids, they needed to live as a family, and not hide the 'wife' in the bush!

Our church was called the First Baptist Church of Mocuba - or in Portuguese, Primiera Igreja Baptista. I have already mentioned about the dear couple that came to live in Mocuba in 2003, named Sam and Kylah Clark-Goff on a two-year assignment. She was gifted in writing poetry. The following poem by Kylah Clark-Goff depicts some of the struggles we had with our church. They were steeped in tradition, and as you will see, the long, hot services were quite a challenge to sit through. Enjoy!

Primeira Igreja Baptista
By Kylah Clark-Goff

It's hot, I'm queasy, and I think it's safe to say
That I'm feeling a bit less than content today.

The AC must have broken - oh yeah - we don't have any!
Concrete walls and a tin roof - what we have is warmth aplenty.

I've been sitting here for hours - I know they speak about our Lord.
But as little as I understand, I'm getting oh so bored.

Here in Primeira Igreja, foreign words fly all around.
I strain to catch one here and there, but mostly it's just sounds.

So we bow our heads to pray "Nosso Deus, nosso Pai" [our Father,
which art in heaven]
But after that I end up lost - even when I try.

The prayer is clearly over when the singing starts anew.
Every aspect of the service claims it's own special tune.

"Visitantes sejam bem-vindos…" We sing this welcome every week.
Visitors we may not have, but in tradition we are steeped.

Announcements and time of offering have their own songs as well-
Evidence of Catholic influence? Is it worship or ritual?

We sing all six verses and they must march in from the back.
We just finished the time of music - after an hour and a half!

Today is a good one. I got a bench that has a back!
Those hours pass more slowly when sitting on grass mats.

A bench by the window is really quite a treat.
A little breeze brings some cool, while pushing smells on past my seat!

Floating through the room: smells of defecation and B.O.
No TP or running water makes me want to hold my nose.

So what's that text the speaker said? Filipenses [Philippians] 4:11
Content in "whatever circumstances"? Surely Paul was jesting!

Or maybe contentedness, Paul learned through years of time.
And pouco pouco [little by little], Sunday by Sunday, maybe so will I.

Isolation

Unless a person has been in a situation like this, one cannot empathize with what it was like to feel so isolated. We felt so cut off from the outside world. Another difficulty was the fact that we were so far from big cities that had grocery stores, butcheries, hospitals, etc. We were two hours from the closest town, Quelimane, and it did have some fairly nice grocery stores and some butcheries, etc. We would go to Quelimane once a month or so to buy groceries. For almost two years, we did not have a phone, so we would drive the two hours with our laptop to download and send our messages. So we would write letters, and put them in the outbox and when we could get to Quelimane, we would send them. (When we first moved to Africa, we had a home phone and e-mail. We started depending on that contact with the outside world and missed it terribly when we moved to Mocuba - because we knew what it was like to have it!) I felt like I never knew what was happening in the world, since we didn't have newspapers, nor could we watch the news.

I must say that not having a phone was a huge problem. I just hated not being able to contact my family. Our neighbors had phones, and I would give my family their numbers if there was an emergency, but when they would need to call us, the phones wouldn't be working. One time, Mike's grandmother had a stroke, and we didn't know about it until two to three weeks later. After that happened, we were blessed with a satellite phone. A church back home bought this for us, and they are very expensive, but we were so grateful. But we still couldn't send e-mails with this phone.

Then one day, the city moved a little metal shipping container to our main street and it was public phones! Now I could go down to this little phone booth and call my family! It was air-conditioned in there - it was heavenly! So one day, I took my laptop and asked the lady if I could please plug my computer in to the phone line. She had never heard of e-mail before. I explained that I still would be paying for the call, as all the phones were metered and you paid per minute. So she asked me where I would be phoning. I explained to her that our e-mail server was in the next city, two hours away in Quelimane. But I had explained to her that I needed to download my messages so I could hear from my family - I was trying to put a guilt trip on her to let me! So then she asked me if my family lived in Quelimane. I explained that my server was in Quelimane, but that the messages were coming from America, and for that matter, could come from all over the world. Well, that just freaked her out, and later she told someone that I was probably a spy and that my laptop was some secret machine! Needless to say, she didn't let me download my messages. Driving a four-hour round trip just to do e-mail is quite hard. Sometimes when we drove the four hours, the server would be down, and we had done the trip in vain.

When we did get a phone, we had a very slow connection and couldn't get onto the Internet. It was very costly to receive pictures because we had to pay per byte that we downloaded. So we told people to please not send us pictures. One day I got a picture and we figured out it cost about $30.00 to download because of the hours that it took. When we finally got the picture, it was of a dog! A friend from high school, 20 years ago, sent me a picture of his dog! I hadn't heard from the guy in 20 years!

I missed hearing from my parents so much during those weeks in between our trips to send and receive. One of the happiest days of my life was finally getting a home phone and being able to e-mail from home. Have you thanked the Lord for your home phone today, and the ability to hook up to the internet?

Quelimane also was where our post office was. It was such a thrill to check our post box, and occasionally we would have a slip that said we had a package! My deep thanks to Sandy Dyson and Ephesus Baptist Church for keeping us stocked those first few years! I don't know what I would have done without those touches of home. It cost a fortune to mail things and I am forever grateful. When one got a package, one had to go to the counter and show them the paper. One would then have to get in one's car and go to the port to get a customs official. He wouldn't have a car, so we would put him in our car and take him to the post office and show him the package. He would open it and examine it and, depending on the contents, charge us. Sometimes it was normal, and other times it was exorbitant. Then after you paid, you had to take the customs man back down to the port! Then you could go home with your package!

One time, the church sent over a bunch of used glasses. This was a wonderful ministry. But the customs officials thought we were going to set up a shop and sell them. They couldn't believe that we would just be giving things away from free. They put a price tag of about $20.00 per glasses, and there were hundreds of pairs. Unfortunately, that was the only package that we had to leave at customs. But I am sure that they were distributed, or sold to those that needed them.

We have many post office stories but one that sticks out in my mind is the day I went and received a birthday present from my Mom. She always decorates things so nicely, and the box was wrapped with a lovely bow on top. I couldn't wait to receive something from her, and tore into the box. In route, the contents had been stolen. Someone had taken the time to unwrap the present, open the box, steal it, and then wrap it back nicely and send it on its way! I will never forget that day when I got the empty box!

When Christmas drew near, I would get so worried that the packages from home were not going to arrive. There were small little things I could have bought the children there in Mozambique, but it was always a treat to have something from America to open on Christmas. I was afraid several years that I would just have to tell the kids that Santa Claus didn't come that year.

So Quelimane was two hours away and Blantyre, Malawi, was six to eight hours away, depending on the road. It was a dirt road, and during rainy season, it was very difficult to drive on. We would go to Blantyre about once a quarter, where there were very nice grocery stores and butcheries. We would buy for three months at a time, and only go to Quelimane for small things. There was a nice hospital in Blantyre, run by the Seventh Day Adventists. This is where I was operated on when I had the spider bite. Timothy got his first glasses in Blantyre, and one could buy medicine and other needed supplies.

But it was still stressful in Malawi. The traffic policemen were very corrupt and would stop you for any thing. One time they stopped us for not having the proper demarkation on our vehicle. In Malawi, they require each car to have stenciled on the side of the car, the name of who the car is registered under, and the carrying weight of the vehicle. This was only a requirement in Malawi, and since we didn't live there, we told the officer that we didn't think the law applied to us. He told us that "When in Rome, do as the Romans do!" When they stopped you, they always asked to see your car registration documents, drivers license, and passport. On this particular day, they walked off with Mike's passport and documents and got in their car and drove away. We began to follow them and that made the officer very mad. He gave us a huge fine, and required us to pay it on the spot. The only way he would give us the documents back was after we showed him the receipt that we paid the fine. You always had to have such a lot of money on you, because you were always getting stopped for things you didn't do. And they had no credit card facilities, of course. Sometimes they had road blocks every few kilometers. Each time they stopped you, your heart went up to your throat. Most of the times, they were just checking to see if your documents were current, but other times they would find anything to fine you for! So getting away for a vacation, even in a nicer country like Malawi, was very stressful!

Johannesburg, South Africa, was a four day drive away. We would go there once a year for medical and dental visits, and for pleasure. We would eat at McDonalds and Pizza Hut and feel we were in heaven! We would always have to get our car fixed, and to buy parts for broken things at home - like washing machine parts or other appliances. At times, we would need to get our computer fixed and other things. There is a very nice Baptist guesthouse and we would go down and stay for two to three weeks at a time. One time during one of our four-day trips, the kids were being extra bad. They were so bored and we kept trying to bribe them. We kept telling them that in just a few more days, or then hours, we would be at McDonalds. We got to the first city in South Africa and went to the mall, practically running to the food court, so excited to be at McDonalds. When we got there, the McDonalds had closed due to lack of business! You talk about some disappointed kids! But luckily when we got to Johannesburg, they had one!

So you can see, we lived a long way from everything. In Mocuba, there really was very little to do. The kids had no school, or lessons, or extra curricular things, unless we organized it ourselves. We had a few restaurants, but it would take sometimes 2-3 hours to be served, as they wouldn't keep food on hand. They would have to go find a live chicken and kill it and go buy the things at that time. It was not worth it usually! There was a fairly nice place, and you would need to go there the day before and order and when you got there the next day, your fish or chicken would be ready. There was definitely no such thing as fast food! One time we were at the restaurant, and of course, all the restaurants had bars. There was a very drunk man that kept coming over to Grace and trying to get her to dance with him, and one time he tried to grab her. Mike kept asking the waitresses to do something, or we were going to leave, and not pay for our food, since it hadn't been brought yet. They did nothing to help, not seeing this as a problem. Every time you ate out, the beggars would stare at you through the window, or even come inside and ask for food. It was very stressful!

We generally handled it fine, but every once in a while, the isolation really got to us. You would just kill to be able to watch TV, buy a newspaper, watch the news, know what is going on in the world, go to a movie, or swim on a really hot day! Mocuba did have a large public swimming pool that was built during the colonial days. It had a high dive and was really very nice, but it hadn't been opened in many years due to the war. Someone tried to rehabilitate it and open it up, but because our water was so dirty from the city, even if they had had the chemicals they needed (which they couldn't get) it would still have been brown. So they tried to open it, and they had those long cleaning poles, and they would get men to always be fishing out leaves and things with those poles. I took the children there, and it was so hot and we were so bored, that they actually enjoyed it. Some of the other missionaries wouldn't let their kids go - there was no telling what diseases you could have pick up from that unclean water (bilharzia waiting to happen)! But we were desperate! But the second time we went, the children were bit underwater by these terrible looking crab-like creatures that have pinching claws! Needless to say, we didn't go back! The one day we were there, it was so crowded, as it was quite a novelty since it hadn't been opened since the Portuguese days. They were selling beer and wine, and everyone was drinking. They would even carry the bottles up on the high dive and drink up there. Needless, to say, we got out of there!

We were always grateful for the other missionaries that would help us. One time there was no peanut butter in the city, and some missionary friends had a surplus, so we could buy from them. Or at other times, when one family would go to Zimbabwe to buy supplies, they would bring treats for other families. I remember one time when a family brought us a bag of Fritos and it was like gold. It was always a blessing when someone went to check the communal post office box and arrive back with something for us. Getting things from home was a lifesaver!

Water and Electricity problems

Due to the war, the infrastructure was very bad. The electricity was sporadic and unreliable. It could be off for days at a time. At times, the voltage would get very low, and you would have a brown out. This could damage your appliances, so when we saw the lights getting very dim, we knew we were having a brownout. We would quickly go and unplug the major appliances that would be affected by the up and down power. Just as the power would get too low, at other times there would be a sudden spike in power. On one of these spikes, we lost a computer, microwave, fans, transformers, etc. On this occasion, the line got crossed, and instead of 220 volts, we had 440 volts. The electricity in our house came from the city and was divided into three lines. So to keep everything working, Mike had it wired so that the major appliances were dispersed over the three phases. Had they all been on one phase, none of them would have worked. One time when installing a water heater, he got electrocuted and the shock went through his heart.

Several times a week, the electricity would only come to one phase or two. So, for instance, if the refrigerator was on the phase that was out, Mike would have to rewire the refrigerator to another phase that was working at the time. I was so grateful to have been married to a handyman! He was amazing at rewiring things to keep everything going, with minimal damage. We also made friends with the people that worked at the electricity company. Many times our large appliances would blow the wires and our electricity would go out. We would have to go down to the electric company, and ask someone to come to our house and rewire the wire at the pole. We would have to give them a lift to our house, and then take them back to work! We are thankful for the generator that we had that we could use for lights and the refrigerator when the power was out. Had we not have had this, we would have lost the goods in our refrigerator many times. When the whole city was dark, it was so nice to be able to watch a video, have lights and have the fan going. Again, Mike had to wire the generator and keep all the appliances wired to it. Mike spent a lot of time just helping us live by keeping things running.

Another problem was water. The city did supply water through the pipes, but most of the time for only a few hours a day. So Mike had to oversee the building of a large cistern in our yard that would collect the water brought by the city each day. If we hadn't have had the cistern, we could only have had water coming out of the tap those few hours. But most of the time, our cistern would have water in it and we had water almost all the time. In the very dry months, the river would run dry at times, and the city would have no water. A few times, we used up all the water in the cistern, and had to borrow a water trailer that belonged to another missionary, and we would have to go buy water to fill our cistern. But the water was very dirty. One could not drink it. When one ran bath water, if was almost like taking a bath in weak tea - it was about that color. The best thing was to take a quick shower and not think about it! Washing your clothes in light brown water eventually turns your clothes a different color. When packing for furlough, most missionaries take very few of their clothes home - they are not fit to wear, and it is a good time to buy new ones!

It was a very demanding job to filter enough water to drink, and to cook with. One had to be thinking of it constantly: to fill containers up with clean water to cook with and drink. On those very hot days, we gave out lots of clean, cold water to people that would come to our gate, or people that came to visit. They had no way to clean their water or make it cold, so drinking cold, clean water was a real treat! They would catch rainwater to drink, but during the dry season, it was such a problem. We were doing what the Bible commands us to do - give a cup of water in His name.

One time I was visiting the prison. There they had no clean water to drink - just the nasty stuff that comes out of the tap - and that was just a few hours a day. One year for Christmas, we took a lot of food and clean, cold water to them on Christmas day. For many months to come, they talked about us coming with that cold, clean water! What a small thing we all take for granted! Have you thanked the Lord for your clean water today?

Several times when Mike was visiting in the outlying areas, he was given water by the host and he thought it was well water. He drank it, thinking it was clean. Each time he got amebic dysentery (diarrhea with blood). After having that a few times, he learned to always bring water from home.

Again, filtering enough water and having water really was something you had to think about often. You couldn't rinse your mouth out with it when you were brushing your teeth, or run your toothbrush under it. When we would go to South Africa on vacation, it was so weird to be able to rinse your mouth out with the tap water! When we would go to a new city, the kids would always ask, "Can we drink this water?"

Several times when Mike was visiting in the outlying areas, he was given water by the host and he thought it was well water. He drank it, thinking it was clean. Each time he got amebic dysentery (diarrhea with blood). After having that a few times, he learned to always bring water from home.

Theft

During our 5-½ years there, we were robbed ten times. Some of them were huge things, and others could be classified as small things. No one ever entered our house to rob us, for which we praise the Lord. Each house worker/maid stole from us- the first lady stole $3,000 worth of items, and others stole less. After this first worker who stole so much, we decided to get a male Bible college student. We had heard the males don't steal as much; whereas the ladies are always trying to provide for their children at home. But, one day I was trying to make up the beds after washing the sheets. I couldn't seem to find any sheets in the linen closet that matched I looked and looked and finally asked our houseworker. He lied at first, but then it was obvious on his face. He told us that since we had two of each kind of sheet, that he had just taken one of each set! I showed him our beds, and how you need two sheets. He was very embarrassed but never brought them back. I have mismatching sheets to this day! From that theft of sheets, it went from bad to worse, and needless to say, he lost his job!

After some time, we got another worker. In more developed countries, people don't have to have maids, but in a country like Mozambique, it is hard to do without one. Since I was home schooling full-time, the worker would help wash clothes, do the dishes, go to the market to buy vegetables, answer all the people at the gate, filter water and clean house. Then they would have to iron all the clothes, due to that little fly that gets on your clothes. After firing the second worker, we decided that maybe if we got a man from our church, he wouldn't steal from us! He was great for several years and really became part of the family. He was one of my baseball coaches and a great friend. But one day as I was setting the table, I realized that I didn't have but two knives! I asked him if he had put them in a different drawer, and again, I could see that although he denied it, he was lying. We began to look around the house and found many things missing- a pillow, books, other dishes, etc. We told him that he could go home and bring them back and then he wouldn't lose his job. But if he didn't bring them back, he would be fired. We kept seeing him in town, and asked if he was going to bring them back.

Finally, one day, we got a summons from the court that he was taking us to court for firing him. The labor court would then expect a settlement from us. Mike explained to the judge that we weren't firing him for nothing, that he had stolen from us! Well, the judge ruled in the worker's favor and we had to pay a lot of money, since he had worked for us for so long. This man was a Christian brother in our church! On the letter he had written to the judge, he called Mike, "Brother Mike", and signed it "Brother Simões". This word, "brother," was a term of endearment - like brothers in the Lord. Needless to say, we were devastated by this violation of trust from a member of our church. He stopped coming to church, took another wife and left the present wife, and we didn't see him much. But even though we tried to forgive, when we saw him in town, I would get a lump in my throat. I think the reason we felt so violated is that he had been in our house - he knew everything about us.

But not one of these workers would have classified what they did as stealing. In their culture, if a person is rich, and has ten knives, for instance, to take eight of them is not stealing. In their eyes, the rich man had too many and he should share. They never felt bad for what they had done. No remorse. It was very difficult to explain this to our children, who saw our workers as part of the family. There is a huge cultural difference in what we consider morally wrong and what they do! To them, to lose your temper and get angry with someone is the worst sin of all. Stealing is not bad to them, but getting angry is! So unfortunately, they did see us get angry, and to them, this is the worst possible sin!

Besides the inside worker, we also had a day guard and a night guard. They were not armed, but just their presence would prevent people from jumping the fence and taking things in our yard. At one time during a crime spree, we hired two night guards so that they could help keep each other awake. I fed the night guards every night, so I knew they got a nice meal. Another one of their jobs was to make the dog food. You couldn't buy commercial dog food (you could at the end of our time there, but it was so expensive). They would cook rice and little dried fish. Most internationals fed their dogs this, as it was good for the dogs, and very inexpensive. But the hard thing is that this is also the food that people would eat for a regular meal. So when we would get a new guard, we would notice that the dogs would be getting skinnier and skinnier. We would find out that the guard was eating what we had bought for the dog! So that is why I fed the guards every night - to keep them from eating the dog food! Also, sometimes the sacks of corn meal and dried fish would be consumed very quickly; we soon discovered they were taking the "dog food" home to feed their families.

We were close to these men as well and many nights would talk to them through the screened door, since we couldn't be outside due to the mosquitoes. (The malaria carrying mosquitoes bite at night). It was always sad when we had to fire guards. Most of the time it was for drinking. They would show up drunk and eventually we would have to fire them. One guard showed up and was acting very strange. He was flirting with me and trying to touch me and he made a pass at me. We realized then he had been drinking. Since Mike was away over night so much, we really depended on these guards. So when we did have problems we would fire them immediately and get another one. When Mike was away, he was depending on these men to keep his family safe. Luckily only that one took us to court for severance pay (after he stole from us!)

Another time we experienced a theft was in Malawi. We had gone there to the international airport to pick up Mike's mother and another dear couple from North Carolina, Rev. and Mrs. Giles. When we picked them up, all but one of their suitcases had arrived. We waited for a day or two, but that one piece of luggage didn't arrive. We had to go back to Mozambique without it, because we had a tight schedule of work and ministry lined up for them. The missionaries in Malawi promised to go pick it up when it arrived and put it in the Baptist guest house. The guest house had a good security system. They had panic buttons in several rooms of the house, and when pushed, an armed group of security guards would arrive within minutes. When we returned to Malawi in two weeks to take them back to the airport, we would get the suitcase then. So during their visit, we heard that it had indeed arrived and we could pick it up on the return trip. The suitcase had some of Les's clothes, but it also had a laptop for us in it. We were so happy to hear that it had arrived safely.

When we got back to Malawi to take them to the airport, we stayed in the Baptist guest house. We stopped by the caretaker's house and got the key and just let ourselves in. When we got in the house, I noticed that there were a few photographs my Mom had sent and a letter and other random things from the suitcase on the table. We couldn't find the suitcase, which the missionaries said was in the room. In a little while, the caretaker came and knocked on our door. He told us what had happened. The missionaries did indeed put the suitcase in the room, and then that night, there had been a robbery. They had broken the suitcase open and ran away with anything of value. They found the pictures and the letter and a few other things in the bushes outside.

Needless to say we were devastated about our laptop. The Giles too had lost valued items. That night we were just sitting around the small living room of the guest house, when we heard a lot of men outside. Eight to ten men busted through the door of the guest house and surrounded us. They had guns and had hoods on to cover their faces. They immediately began to tell us that they were the security company; that they were the good guys. They were looking in every room and yelling and we were absolutely traumatized. We kept asking them who they were, and they kept saying they were from the security company, but they looked like bad guys to us! We didn't believe them. We hadn't called them by pushing the panic button. After they looked in every room and all outside, they ran away. We ran outside to find the caretaker. He told us that he had pushed the security button to see if the service was activated - because obviously, during the robbery the previous night, the guards/police hadn't come. So without telling us, he pushed the security button that calls the rapid response team. So they came in, not knowing that it was a trial. They came in looking for an armed group of bad guys. Needless to say, we did not sleep much that night. After an almost perfect trip with Mrs. Boone and the Giles, I am afraid that the memories of this traumatic experience on the last night of their African journey stayed with them!

The last year we were in Mozambique, we came to our annual Prayer Retreat in South Africa. We were in a lovely resort and the real treat was that my parents were there. My father was the speaker at the daily worship services that we had with all the missionaries. We were sharing a room with them. One day, Mike went back to the room to get something he had forgotten. He noticed that our room was in disarray! There were potato chips all over the floor, black footprints, and everything topsy-turvy. He came quickly to where I was and said that something had happened in our room and that I must come with him. I immediately began to think that we had been robbed, like all the other times! Upon close inspection, we realized that this chaos was not the work of a person, but a baboon! We knew that there were baboons in the area, and that occasionally they would climb through the window and wreak havoc! He didn't like that flavor of potato chips and dumped them all over the floor! He took those little containers of coffee creamer that have the little pull-back top, and he had drank the milk and left all the containers on the floor! We had a very good laugh, and decided to close our windows after that. But since we had been robbed so often, we just assumed it had happened again!

So even after ten times, it never got any easier to be stolen from. For days afterwards, you feel violated and relive the experience over and over. But we are grateful for the Lord's protection over all our possessions and that not more was taken.

Poverty

When we moved to Mozambique in 1998, it was listed as the poorest country in the world, and one of the highest in terms of human suffering. It had two million land mines. It was common to see land-mine victims with one leg or one arm. It would be fairly normal to see a man with one leg riding a bike. There were many birth defects that you knew could have easily been fixed, had they had a proper hospital. You never got used to the beggars, especially the little children that would follow you everywhere. You never got used to the fact that we seemed to have so much, and they had so little. It was not nice to always be judged as a "rich person." The nationals rarely saw us as having any needs, because to a hungry person, we had everything. I would try to be honest with them

and I told them about some of our struggles- with sickness, theft
and homesickness. But I could tell from their reaction that they
really didn't think I had any needs or pain.

The hunger was all around you. We would see the nationals
set a field on fire in a controlled burn, so that the rats would run
out of the field, and they could eat them. One of the first things
you noticed when entering Malawi was the people standing on
the sides of the road selling shiskabobbed rats on a stick. People
would laugh and call it "Malawi fast-food", but I sure didn't think
it was funny. We could never come to peace with the dichotomy
between the rich and poor. One time we got steaks from Malawi
and drove back with them the seven hours to Mocuba. As Mike
grilled them outside on the grill, we realized so many people were
watching us, as we had a very low fence around our house. It was
very difficult to sit there and be grilling steaks with some of the
poorest people in the world staring at you. We were very generous
and were always giving things away and helping people with food,
clothes and medicine, but of course, we couldn't feed and help the
whole town, so we always felt guilty when we had to say no. This
will be one question I will ask the Lord in heaven- why some people
in the world have it so easy, and others are eating rats. It cannot be
that the prosperous nations are like they are because they deserve
it, and the poor are like they are because they deserve it. So many of
the poor in the world are dear, and do also deserve better, but there
are too many things going against them – war, natural disasters,
corrupt governments, etc.

The hunger around us continued to really affect us. One night
after we were locked inside, we heard all this commotion outside.
It is always scary to hear these things, as one doesn't know if there
are political riots, or what. Then when we looked outside we saw
all these people in our yard. It was terrifying! They were jumping
and screaming and our night guards were trying to control them.
We screamed to our guard to please tell us what was happening.
He told us the people were collecting these huge grasshoppers
that migrated to Mocuba each year. Because we had such bright,
powerful security lights, they were attracted to the light! We went
outside and saw these huge bugs flying into the light. It was like
the plague had hit our yard! The people were catching the bugs and
putting them in their pockets and taking off their wrap-around

skirts to tie them up. Others asked us for plastic bags so they could please take them home. They said they were delicious cooked, and that they were hungry. I just thought that was so sad! It happened each year during their migration!

The long standing war in Mozambique led to the immense poverty. They are busy trying to blow up all the land mines, but it is a very costly and dangerous job. It costs $3.00 to manufacture and plant a landmine, and $1,000.00 to remove it. Thus you can see why still to this day there are over 1 million underground. The human cost is one that can't be measured. They say that 20 people per month step on landmines and that 60% of them die due to lack of medical care. One day while Mike was returning back from a church visit, he saw that the road was blocked with the big mine removal operation. They came and blocked him from passing, saying that they were busy blowing up a mine. In a few minutes, he heard a loud boom, and then they came to him and said that he could pass.

Bread was a big staple in Mozambique. It was very Portuguese to have these hard little rolls as a meal. Many times as you were eating bread, you would bite down on something grainy and there would be kind of a crunch, and you would realize it was sand. There was a bakery in town that made the little rolls. I was looking for a field trip to take Tim and Grace on, so I asked the man that owned the bakery if we could tour it and see how it was made. Left over from colonial days, they had a huge mixer that sat on the floor and nice wood-baked ovens. When we got to the bakery, they told us that to make the flour go further, they add sand!

To see children so behind developmentally was also very challenging. When we went to the many churches in the outlying areas, we would take crayons and Bible coloring pages to the children. Many children, even young teenagers would not know how to hold a crayon, or what to do with it.

The Three C's- Communism, Corruption, and Catholicism

The three C's listed above also greatly affected our work. Mozambique had been a Communist country and we felt its affects everywhere. There was the feeling that no one could rise above his fellow countryman, so we saw the lack of motivation or desire to succeed. When you entered a little shop in town, many times you felt like you were bothering them by coming in to buy something! There wasn't the attitude that you must be friendly in order to gain more customers.

I think the local police and officials didn't quite know what to do with us white missionaries. The Portuguese had left years ago, and there had been very few white people in the country and they were not sure of our motives. You always sensed that they really didn't want you there. It was never this attitude of "thank you very much for coming to help my country."

There was a missionary in Mocuba named Antonio. He was a Mozambican, but had been trained as a missionary with Operation Mobilization. He had served for several years on the missionary ship, the Doulos, and had traveled the world. He had moved back to the city of his birth after his assignment on the ship. One day, the police stopped him. They asked him what all these white missionaries were doing in his city. They had seen white children on bicycles riding through the city. They said that this made them nervous-because usually the UN and aid workers were single men or single women. And they knew that they had a very short assignment. But when they saw white children, like Timothy and Grace, they felt like that was a sign that we were planning on staying and raising our families there. They told Antonio that he must personally take responsibility for all the white missionaries; he had to vouch for them. If any of us got out of line, or did anything against the country, he would be to blame. Luckily, he took that responsibility!

Corruption was the second problem. They wouldn't have signs on the road telling the speed limit, but they would give you a ticket for speeding. And sometimes the price of the fine would be exorbitant! They would give tickets for anything: wearing sunglasses over a bridge, or transporting a board that stuck out of the back of your truck (even though their public taxis would have people hanging out, and goats and pigs tied everywhere). We got tickets for having our car lights on in the daytime, and because our truck's canopy wasn't registered. Our truck came from Japan and it arrived without a canopy. So when it arrived, the mission registered it. So it was registered without a canopy. But then we got a canopy put on so we could transport things safely in the back.

So they gave us a ticket and we had to pay a huge fine because we had added a canopy, and it wasn't registered with one!

You had to have a license and a permit to drive a bicycle, and we got tickets for not having that. You had to have three orange emergency triangles in your vehicle. For a long time, the law was two triangles, which we had. Then they stopped us and charged us a fine for not having three! If you tried to talk to them about these unfair rules, they would take your passport and Mozambican identity document and say they were going to keep it! You knew you couldn't allow that, so you would just have to pay it.

The next "C" is Catholicism. To all my Catholic brothers and sisters, please hear me out. Most of the Mozambicans in our area were cultural Catholic. They rarely went to mass, but if you asked them what church they went to, or if they were Christians, they would say they were Catholic. They therefore did not sense their need of God, since they were already "religious". The church would endorse ancestral worship and allow the people to participate in the ceremonies to contact their ancestors. If they were practising Christians, that would have been one thing, but most weren't. It was the state church, and to be Mozambican, was to be Catholic. When I started doing a Bible study with some Catholic youth, they were so happy to hear and study the Bible. They said they had never done that in their church. Again, it is easier when people don't have a "religion" than when they "think" they do.

Traveling

In mentioning the difficulties of living in Mozambique, the one that also ranks right up there is the dangers associated with travel. Traveling was always difficult due to the effects of the war. Many roads and bridges had been destroyed and others washed away by floods. Many of the main roads in Mozambique are dirt roads that were poorly made and poorly maintained. Even the paved roads are so cracked up and broken, that it would be better to have the dirt roads than the old paved ones. The potholes in many roads were so big your whole car could go in them. The other problem was the deep sand. One would be driving on it and then suddenly start sinking. We often got stuck in the sand. On one of my first days in Mocuba, I decided to take the kids to town get a cold Coke. I went down a side street that had washed away due to rain and neglect during the war, and I literally fell in a huge hole. It is a miracle that we were not injured. I luckily had met a South African businessman and happened to be near his house. He came and pulled us out!

Another time I got stuck in the sand while I was at church. At this time, we didn't have a 4 x 4. As I tried to reverse out of the space in front of the church, my car just sunk in the sand up to the bumper. It was quite funny how many Africans came to see the three white ladies stuck in the sand. They all got to digging, putting bricks under the wheel, and then about 50 of them tried to pick it up. We finally had to send word to a missionary in town to come get us. He had to lift the car up with his hydraulic jack and then pull it out with a chain.

I personally got stuck many times - either in the deep sand because it was so dry, or the wet mud when it had rained a lot. Remember, many of the churches are in the bush. Our second truck was a 4 X 4, and when we would get stuck we would have to get out of the car and lock the tires. Most of the time, Mike was driving and he got very good at getting us unstuck, and also changing the many, many flat tires we had. But many times I would drive alone to go teach literacy and I would always panic when I got stuck. Because there were no cell phones, I would always worry I wouldn't get home before dark and would have to sleep there, and there was no way to get word to Mike! So on a little piece of paper, Mike wrote me the instructions on what to do when I got stuck:

1. DON'T PANIC
2. Get out and lock the front tires.
3. Put the 4 x 4 gear shift in H4, and the transmission gear shift in neutral.
4. If you need more power, put it in L4.
5. After the danger has passed, RELAX

Then after that, there were three more steps in how to put it back the way it was! People were always around to help, and I was never afraid that anyone would hurt me while I was stuck - the local church people would see to that.

We didn't have cell phones and literally trusted God for every trip. We began to pray before we even left our driveway. There were always animals and people in the roads. You never drove at night, because there were few streetlights. Children played in the roads and were never afraid of cars. Most people rode on bicycles, and they were all over the road, also dodging the potholes. You have already read of how the little child hit Mike's trailer, and he thought he was dead. The people had no fear of cars and would literally walk right out in front of you.

Then you had the problem of drunk people. One day, Mike was coming back from a church visit. When I use the term "church visit", I want you to picture what that means. The churches were many times in the center of the villages. Because most of the people didn't work, they would be home working in their gardens, or grinding corn, etc. When Mike would pull up in his truck, all the people around the church, even for miles around, would gather. He would teach them, and they would sing and worship together. Sometimes he would show the JESUS film, or have times when they would reach out in to the community to those that didn't come to church. He would also have a time of training with the leaders and discuss other church problems or issues. They would eat together, and many times he would sleep in his tent at the church and stay for several days.

As he was returning late one Sunday afternoon, just at dusk, a drunken man riding a bicycle pulled out in front of him on the main road. He was looking ahead, and saw the man, and he slowed down and came to a complete stop while the drunken man got off the road. But just as Mike was starting to go again, the drunken man crossed back in front of his truck, and Mike unavoidably hit him. The bike was damaged, but the drunken man was completely oblivious to what had happened and was not injured. Crowds gather immediately when something like this happens. The crowds many times get violent, as they see someone in their tribe that has been injured, and they feel it is always the motorist's fault. They are also so poor, that they are looking for a way for the blame to go to the motorist, so they can get a payout, or a new bike, or whatever. It clearly was not Mike's fault, but he was terrified at the approaching crowd gathering around his vehicle. At times, they can begin to stone the person or injure them in some way. Immediately, from out of the crowd, a nice man came up to Mike. He noticed the sign that was always on our truck that said we worked with the Baptist Mission. So he immediately said that he was a Baptist from another city, and that he knew the other Baptist missionary, John, who lived two hours away. This man was educated and told Mike he would handle the whole situation. He began to write an official report about what had happened. He did figure that Mike would have to pay to buy the man a new bike, as his bike was quite damaged. He wrote up the report and had Mike and another witness sign it. Mike paid a little bit of money, and then the man told Mike to leave immediately, so as not to incite more of a riot. Mike is still convinced this man was an angel - he came from nowhere, was a Baptist, knew the other missionary, was educated and had a notebook with him, was well respected by the crowd, etc. God is so good! We never saw him before or after the incident! We still don't know who this man was!

Here is another example of the dangers on the Mozambican roads. Mike was to drive to another city called Cuamba. It was about eight hours away. He was to meet another missionary named David there. David was coming from the north, and Mike was coming from the south, and they were to meet there and do some ministry together, as there was no missionary that lived in Cuamba – which was quite a strategic city. They had made a plan of where to meet - but of course, neither of them had cell phones. Mike left early that morning with just a little bit of clean water and just one snack, because he knew in 8 hours, he would be in this city, and he would be cared for by the Baptist church. But 9 miles away from Cuamba, a huge bus had overturned because the road to Cuamba had been washed away. He tried to cross another bridge, but it was flooded and he couldn't pass. He absolutely had no way to get the message to David that he had tried and was just 9 miles away, but he couldn't get there! The problem was that he then had to return the 8 hours to get home. He was also going to fill up the gas tank in Cuamba. So 16 hours later he drove up at home, and I was so surprised to see him, as he wasn't supposed to be home for days. Starving and thirsty, he told me the story. But God's grace was so sufficient to make his gas last the whole trip. What a horrible day, but things could have been worse - he could have run out of gas on those long stretches of deserted roads.

As I have said, the traveling situation was made worse in that the infrastructure in this war-torn country had been destroyed. Bridges and roads and train tracks were destroyed by one side or the other. They had built some new bridges to replace the old, blown up ones, but they didn't remove the incomplete ones. Many times you would see bridges that would just drop off in mid air. Usually there were signs warning you of these upcoming incomplete, blown-up bridges, but other times there weren't. It is just God's grace that people don't just go driving off those! The bridges that were there also didn't have guardrails. We knew of several accidents when people slid off the bridges and died from the huge fall. Traveling was also dangerous because of the remoteness of our work, and because of the huge distances we had to travel to cover our job assignment To get to many of our churches was an adventure. The scariest thing would be when the church would make a bridge for us to cross over a stream in the path to drive to their church. They would cut down these huge trees (of course, with no electrical saws or machinery), and they would secure them in the ground by hand. For our car to drive over, they knew they needed about 6-7 large trees. I never got comfortable driving over those hand-made bridges. The only good part was that if we fell, the distance wasn't huge, and we probably wouldn't have died. We might have died from a heart attack when the log gave way, but we wouldn't have plummeted too far! Sometimes I must admit I would walk over the bridges while Mike drove!

So to get to every one of the 100 churches there were challenges in travel. None of the roads were marked, and there were no maps, so you just had to know which dirt path to turn down. To get to one church in Lugela, I would have to take Mike to the river in Mocuba near our house and drop him off on our side of the river with his bike. (The bridge had been washed away). He would get into a canoe with his bike and cross the river. Then a public taxi would pick him and many others up from the other side of the river, and he would tie his bike on top of the taxi. He would ride in the taxi for several hours, and then get off in the city of Lugela. Then he would ride his bike down the dirt paths to the church! Then to come home, he would do all that in reverse - bike, taxi, canoe and then bike home!

During rainy season, things were really bad and dangerous. Mike got stuck so many times in the mud and the nationals would have to pull him out. Other times, the roads would be completely impassable, and he would return home unable to make his appointments. Many times our truck would be completely covered in mud when he got back from a church visit. We never understood why people would want to go four-wheeling in the mud, like you see on TV sometimes - Mike did that often!

Probably one of the worst things for me about Mozambique, when you think of the country as a whole, is that it is divided almost into two countries by the Zambezi River. There is no bridge across it - just an old, unreliable ferry. So progress is greatly hindered in that goods and supplies from the capital must cross this river to get to the north! The ferry would be so crowded, that sometimes trucks would be in a line for 4-5 days. And at the ferry, there was no electricity or hotels. There were just little huts where you could get nationals to make you some food, but no nice restaurant or anything. The north of the country would always complain that their hospitals didn't have medicines, or anything like the south did, but everything had to be transported across this major river!

We had to cross it several times; so therefore we have several ferry stories. One time, on Christmas Eve, we waited in the line for the ferry for nine hours. (My parents were meeting us in South Africa for a vacation on Dec 28, so we had to start our drive on the 24th to get there in time). We used up all our cold water and were literally scared to death that we would die of thirst after that. Remember, Christmas is the hottest time of the year! It was about 100 degrees and people's tempers were flaring, as people would try to jump in ahead of others in line. The people that own the ferry take a long lunch break. So if you arrive during siesta time from 12:00-2:00, just know that the ferry is not going to be working during that time! Often, as well, the ferry breaks, and you have to wait for hours while the ferry is being fixed. So between the long lines, the lunch breaks, and the ferry breaking down, it is really a wonder anyone gets across! We finally got across after nine hours, on the last ferry of the day! There was so much anger that I was really afraid someone would get killed trying to get across that river on Christmas Eve. People kept breaking in line, and it was definitely not first come, first served!

Since we had waited for nine hours, this meant that we were very far from where we were to spend the night that evening. We thought we would cross the ferry early in the morning, and then drive all day to get to a missionary farm that night. But by the time we crossed the ferry, and drove to where we had a place to stay, it was midnight! It is always very dangerous to drive at night, but we had no choice. They were repairing the road on the other side of the ferry, and they would repair it section at a time. While they were repairing a certain section, they would detour you down to the side of the road, down an incline. But it was dark, and had been raining, and several times we slid down the embankments, and one time we almost flipped the car. It went over on two wheels, but Mike was able to take control and get it down. We ended up arriving in the city where we were to spend the night at 11:30 p.m. We tried to find that missionary farm where we had reservations with. In the dark, we tried and tried, but were unsuccessful. Luckily we knew a Southern Baptist family that lived 45 minutes away from this main road. So at midnight, on Christmas Eve, we rang the doorbell of this family! Their night guard came out and let us in, and the family was still up celebrating Christmas. They took us in, like family, and gave us a nice place to sleep. They fed us, as our food had long run out, and there are no fast food places on the side of the road! So 18 hours after we had left our house, we were safe in an American's home.

Another time we crossed the ferry, we had to wait again. Grace was passionate about birds at this time, and we had been given two hand-raised, tame birds. So in the back seat were the two birds. But the heat at the ferry was so bad, that the birds began to gasp for air, and stop breathing, and faint! Of course, when you are riding down the road, we had the AC on, and this kept them cool, or you could roll down the windows and get a breeze. But when you are stopped at a riverbank, in a long line there is no shade, no fans or anything. People would literally crawl under their cars to get out of the 100+ degrees, and there was no breeze. I got some paper and started fanning those birds and tried to keep them alive. Luckily our wait this time was just a few hours, and not the nine like the previous trip. Had it been nine hours, we would have been burying those birds! And Grace would have been devastated!

When one ferry was broken, there was another ferry about three hours away that was hand-pulled and wasn't supposed to break. So, one time, after seeing the huge long line and after waiting for several hours at the first ferry, we decided to go try the other ferry. So we drove the three hours to it. During that three-hour trip, we had a flat tire, and our AC went out. By the time we got to the second ferry, we found out that the river where the ferry was had flooded and the ferry couldn't operate. So we had to go the three hours back, with no AC to the other ferry and wait in line! Mike rarely breaks down, but as he changed yet another flat tire, he just told me he couldn't go another inch. This was after we had already driven for three days from South Africa! He was at a breaking point. We made it back to the other ferry, and again, got across on the very last trip for the day. If we hadn't made it, we would have had to spend the night in our car. Luckily, we never had to do this, but many of our missionary friends did!

The maddening part of all of this is that money has been given to the Mozambican government to build the bridge across the Zambezi! And the money has mysteriously disappeared. So whoever is behind this corruption is to blame for the top of the country being almost totally cut off from the progress in the south. Every time I saw the South African products in our little stores in Mocuba, I knew they had come by truck across that rickety, dangerous ferry! Many times the chocolate bars from South Africa in the stores, would be in terrible shape - as they had obviously melted in the 4-day journey. Also, the ice cream would be inedible, because of the journey that it had traveled. The Indian businessmen would often travel to South Africa to buy goods to sell up in our city - no wonder the prices would have to be so high. They had driven the four days, plus waited no telling how long, at the ferry.

We hear that now there are two ferries in operation, and when one goes on lunch break, the other runs. We have also heard that there are nice hotels at the ferry now, and even a swimming pool! But it was as I have described it until 2003, so progress came slowly.

It was always amazing to see how God would give grace to handle each situation. One time, while we were at the ferry for nine hours, one of the Mozambican families that had a little house at the ferry would run a little restaurant and cook French fries, or chicken for the many hundreds of people that were waiting. One of these families had a little puppy. This is very rare for Mozambicans - dogs are not valued in their culture, and many times are mistreated, and would just look terrible. They would be tick and flea invested, and just be skin and bones. They would never give a dog, food, because they were too poor themselves. Dogs were just left to scavenge. But this family had the cutest little puppy, well fed, and tied on a little string. He had a water bowl and food bowl right where he was tied. We had never seen that before too - a bowl for the dog's food and water! Grace loved dogs, and she became fascinated with that little puppy. While we waited in line for nine hours, she played with that little dog - taking him for walks and getting him more food and watching him do tricks! I just knew that God had provided this little dog for Grace to be entertained for nine hours. It had to be God, because this was not normally part of Mozambican culture.

If one chose to not go the route of the ferry, one had the option of going another way. Instead of going straight south from Mozambique to South Africa, one could go the long way, passing through several different countries. Since many times one would have to wait a very long time for the ferry, it sometimes worked out to be as quick to go around. If you went around, you would have to cross eight border posts! At each border posts, you had to all get out of your car, and go in to the customs/immigration building. You would have to fill out paper work, saying why you were leaving or entering, and give all the details of your passports and visas and address, etc. You would pay money to leave one country and pay money to enter another country. (Plus you had to have the correct currency as each of these four countries used completely different money). You would then get your passports stamped. Then you would have to fill out more paper work on your vehicle - giving all the registration numbers and license plates, etc. You would pay again for your vehicle to leave one country and enter another. Then you would have to go through a search of your car by the custom's officials. If they saw huge amounts of things that you were going to then turn around and sell in your country, you would have to pay import taxes on that. Many times the guards and officials at the border posts would be drunk, and at times it would be scary.

We were never transporting goods to be sold, but we did buy in huge bulk for our own family when we traveled to more progressive countries. We would stock up on groceries and meat to last for 3-6 months, depending when we would be able to get out again. So many times the officials thought we were going to sell the goods, because there would be so many of them. There were always rules about importing things - like if you imported parts;

you had to pay 100% importation fees. So they were always looking for ways to make lots of money from you. We weren't trying to be dishonest, but we would hide things that we had bought all over the car - behind the seat, etc. It wasn't our fault that they didn't have washing machine parts in our country! We would always have food with us to give the border control guards, and many times, if we would just give them a muffin, they would wave us on through. We would always have to pray before we got to the borders, because you never knew what to expect. Many times they would just ask for a Bible, when they saw we were importing boxes of Bibles, and we were happy to give them one of those. We have had so many miracles at border posts - bringing things we needed into the country, and knowing that they could have charged a huge import duty.

The only illegal thing we did was bring Grace's birds in to the country, and then when we moved, we smuggled them back out! You aren't supposed to bring plants or animals across borders. There is always the chance that they would be disease-carrying. Grace loved her birds, and to get them across legally, would have been a mission! So we covered their cage with a towel, and just prayed a lot, both taking them in and bringing them out. Sometimes they could make you exit the car and do a complete check of the things inside your car, but both times we were smuggling the birds, they didn't! Our prayer was that the birds wouldn't decide to start singing!

We only had two frightening border crossings. One time in Zimbabwe, the border control man was drunk. Zimbabwe has for years been going through a very difficult time economically. They have great difficulty in getting food and fuel in to their country. They are completely bankrupted financially. At this one time, when we were traveling, they were without cooking oil and sugar in the country. As we were traveling through Zimbabwe on the way back from South Africa, we were loaded down with groceries, but honestly didn't have any oil or sugar. We could easily get those in our city, so we didn't take up precious space with things we could get locally. But this man was insistent that in all those boxes of food and supplies, there had to have been sugar and oil. He made us unpack everything, and then he did a search of the inside, even grabbing my purse and going through it. It was quite frightening.

But finally he got so frustrated and he let us go, but we were there a very long time.

The other frightening experience was also at the Zimbabwe border. When one enters the border post, one has to get a form and fill out all your details. Well, when we got to the border, this nice man handed us a form and was helping us fill it out. We just assumed he worked there, since he handed us the form. He took all this time telling us the quickest way to get through all the red tape and showing us where to stand in line. Many times I would wait in the car with Tim and Grace, because they were small and it was quite intimidating to be at these crowded borders. But this man came and told us we must all stand in line, so we obeyed. When we finished, he asked us for a huge fee for his services. Then we realized that this guy was a con artist. When I realized this, I went out to the car, since I wasn't needed. At that time, I saw three men surrounding the car and fixing to break in. They were all a crime ring - the man inside kept the people busy and talking, while his three friends broke into their cars outside. He was determined to get his fee, and kept following us, and we thought we would never get rid of him and get over that border. We went to the officials to see if they could help us get rid of him, and they said that it was our fault that we enlisted his services and we deserved it! But we were totally innocent to his ploy.

Crossing border posts was just a way of life for us, and all the missionaries have their border posts stories of traumas that have happened to them. To get to South Africa, we could either go through Mozambique and cross the ferry, or we could go through Malawi and Zimbabwe to get there. At times we would go one way, and at other times, after bad ferry experiences, would go the other way! To get to South Africa from our house, we would drive six hours to get to Malawi, and there we would have to go through two border posts - the one at which we were leaving Mozambique, and then the one at which we were entering Malawi. Then we would drive for a while, and we would have to then leave Malawi, and go back in to Mozambique. (If you look on the map, Malawi is a small country, and part of it is actually in the middle of Mozambique.) Then we would drive for a while, and would leave Mozambique and go in to Zimbabwe. Then we would drive for a while, and would leave Zimbabwe and go into South Africa.

So, eight times,we would have to do all the things that I mentioned above - forms, money, documents stamped, custom check, etc! This would take four days! Our passports are so thick, as we have had to get extra pages for all the border stamps. One can just get weary looking at our passport, and realizing how many miles and countries have been logged!

Most times we were pretty nervous at the borders, since we never knew how long the line would be, or what they would ask us. But one time, God really did a miracle at a border post. We were entering South Africa, and were at the border. Since so many people leave Mozambique and travel to South Africa (since the economy is better in SA), there is a lot of crime between the two countries. There are huge signs on the sides of the road there that say, "Do not stop on the side of the road. Hijack area. If you have a flat, don't stop!" So when we got out at the border station, and we were walking to our car, we realized our tire was flat! Had it been flat just five 5 minutes before or after, we would have been in danger! So we changed it there safe, with so many police and officials around. We found out later that on the day that we had the flat tire at the border, our family had been mentioned on the CompassionNet website. I had asked for prayer for this long journey, and again, God was faithful to answer the prayer of His saints.

As I said, traveling was very difficult for me. Due to the road conditions, we would have so many flat tires. It was common to lose three tires on a trip. Mike got so tired of changing tires! Then it was just that fear of not knowing what would happen. Then there was the inconvenience of not having any bathroom facilities on the way, or food. And you couldn't step off the road due to the land mines, so we all got used to relieving ourselves right on the road. (Most times they were deserted and no one was watching!) Then there was the added pressure of two small children saying "I'm bored!" We would just pray and get in the car, and have to trust the Lord for our very lives. One day, as we were traveling, I started singing "Amazing Grace" to occupy the time. I sang all the verses, and as I got to the words, "Tis grace has brought us safe thus far, and grace will lead us home", the Lord spoke so clearly to me through those words! He said, "Amy, I have brought you safe thus far, and I *will* lead you home." I know the songwriter was writing about heaven in this song, but to me, home was Mocuba. God so clearly said to me that He had cared for us in the past, and He would lead us home. After that, I would say those words every time I got in the car!

Witchcraft and Spiritual Warfare

In our western worldview, it is very hard for us to understand the religion of the majority in Africa, African Traditional Religions - ATR. The main components of ATR involve animism and ancestral worship. Animism is the belief that everything in nature has a soul. In ancestral worship, when a person dies, they become an ancestor and the ancestors are the ones that control day-to-day life. They have authority over those still living. Most Africans that practice ATR's believe in a Higher Power. They believe God is the creator, but he is not involved in day-to-day life. To them, there are no natural events without a spiritual cause, thus there are no such things as *accidents*. If something bad happens to you, it is because of a spell cast by someone else, or the result of something you have done to upset the ancestors. Thus, sacrifices must be made to keep them happy. Even in times of hunger when their stored up food has run out, before the annual crops came in, they would still make food and brew traditional beer, and put it at the gravesite for the ancestor to eat. In a place of such hunger, I was always amazed at how much food they would prepare and leave on the graves of their ancestors. This food was just wasted. I never understood why they would do that, because unless the food was stolen by someone, they should realize by now that the ancestors don't need the food, because it would still be there week after week! They would commune with the ancestors and they would actually come and tell us what message the ancestors had given to them. They would have very vivid dreams, and they would hear the ancestors speak to them during these dreams. Many times they lived in fear that what they dreamed would come true.

Funerals are a very important occasion to these that practice ATR. A proper burial with the appropriate rights is believed to be necesssary in order for the deceased person to achieve "ancestorhood" or become a spiritual being. After the funeral, shrines are created for those that have died. The people believe that through prayer and sacrifice, they can communicate with their dead family members.

Thus many Africans live a life consumed with fear. They feel they never know if they have done something to upset the ancestors. They always have to wonder if they have done everything they need to do to appease the ancestors. Even after they've accepted Christ this thought is always in the back of their minds. They live in total fear of someone putting a curse on them - thus the need for the traditional ceremonies. They spend a lot of time singing and chanting and beating the drums, consulting with the ancestors to keep themselves protected from evil. Their lives are controlled by pleasing the spirits of their ancestors. The evil spirits would especially bother them at night. They would have terrible nightmares. Some times when I would ask the Mozambicans how they were, they would tell me that the spirits visited them in the previous night and being terrified, they didn't sleep.

They have great fear that life on earth is ruled by forces that make life unsafe for all. This is where witchcraft comes in. Since life to them is unsafe and ruled by evil forces, they feel that they must constantly be prepared for an onslaught. They prepare themselves by wearing protective charms and amulets that they get from the witchdoctor. They spend a lot of money in acquiring charms which they wear as necklaces or waistbands. Besides the ones worn on the body, others are hung on door lintels, while others have things buried under the threshold of the entrance to the house to protect them against invading spirits. The job of parents, they feel, is to ensure that their children are well protected from the evil spirits by putting charms on them. In this witchcraft, spells and curses are done. If people are good at communing with the ancestors, they are given by the tribe the job of being a witchdoctor. We believe that these people are being used by Satan, and are demon-possessed people. You can't play with fire, without getting burned!

They also buried things in their yard with the hope that this would bring them protection, and cause the land around their home to be fertile. One day, Mike and our helper, Antunus were clearing the garden next to our house to get it ready to plant. Our helper stumbled across a plastic bucket buried two feet in the ground. It had been placed upside down, and inside of it was a figurine wrapped up. Antunus was startled and immediately became faint. He got so physically sick that he had to be sent home for the day. The next day, he came back to work, and he and Mike burned the shrine. Antunus never was able to explain to us what it was, or why it had such an effect on him. He said it could have been there for protection, or it could have been placed there as a curse. Antunus was a lovely Christian who seemed to of put ancestor worship behind him. But for some reason, finding this shrine was deeply upsetting to him. This just shows the power of this worldview.

In Mozambique, many times we heard about the *chupa-sangue* (blood sucker). This is what they believed about him: he was a little man that had a very long tube that would come to their house at night. He would throw the very long tube on the roof of their houses - right at the point where the thatched roof peaks. The tube would then be inserted in their arm and he would draw all their blood out. They would come to our house with bruised arms and cuts and tell us that the *chupa-sangue* had come to them last night and sucked all their blood out. Many times, they would have nightmares and feel attacked by the bad spirits at night. The local hospital also would give out false information and this added to this belief. When the lab would do a blood test, and the person was low in iron, they would tell them "they had no blood." So then they believed that someone had sucked their blood out, if they 'didn't have any blood'. No amount of teaching that we did changed this belief! At other times they would wake up with scratches or sores on their arms and legs. They would come and show us and tell us that a mysterious spirit came and did that while they slept.

This worldview is so entrenched in the lives of the people that neither intellectual sophistication nor over a century of Christianity has made a decisive inroad in these practices. The problem we would face is that when people would convert to Christianity, they would still want to trust in their ancestors as well - they would add Christ to the list of people that could help them in this evil world. This is called syncretism - when two belief systems are joined together, but are actually at odds with each other. It is then crucial to teach that God is near to them and that he is interested in their daily lives. They have to know that He wants a relationshp with them through his son Jesus.

Some of you reading may wonder why one cannot just leave Africans alone and let them believe what they have always been taught. People said that to us as we left to go to Africa. We have always told Africans that we are not here to change their culture; we are not trying to make them adopt our Western culture. But each of us has to put our culture up against the Word of God and see if it measures up, or if some things need to be changed. We would always tell them that there are many good things about their culture - the way they are so family oriented, and their respect for their elders - just to give you two examples. We told them that, as Americans, we must put our culture as well up against the Bible and see if there is anything we must change. I must say the way many in the West get consumed with materialism, would be something that we must analyse to see if it is what God wants.

In concluding this section on difficulties, I would like to give you a few examples of the witchcraft and animism that the people so believed in and how it affected us personally.

1.   The first I would call the "owl story". The Lomwe people believed very deeply that if an owl came to your house, it was an omen that bad things were going to happen to you. It was a fairly rare occasion, so they placed great significance in its meaning. Late one night, an owl was heard in the tree right by our back door. The next morning, the night guard, very animatedly, told us that something terrible was going to happen to us soon. Mike shared with him, that those were not our beliefs, and that God was in control, not an owl! The following day was when Mike had the accident in which the drunken man pulled out in front of him and he hit him. When Mike got home that night, he told the guard about his terrible day. Mike was not even thinking about the owl and the prediction the guard had made. The guard said, "I told you so!" Mike was able to tell him that it was a coincidence, and that even if Satan meant to harm Mike, God would use it for the good. He was able to tell him about the miracle of the man just appearing out of nowhere, when the mob began to form and how he calmed the crowd and wrote up the affidavit of what happened. He told how the man was not injured. He was able to tell the guard and show him that God can bring good out of a bad situation. Our guard was a very strong Christian, but believed strongly in the

omen and power of the owl. First John 4: 4 says, "Greater is He that is in you, than he that is in the world".

2. The leaders of the various churches with which we worked were always aware of spiritual oppression. One night, while Mike was camping out after a revival meeting, they were sensing danger. When Mike woke up, he saw that all the leaders had formed a circle around his tent. When he stepped out to relieve himself in the middle of the night, they all instantly woke up. They were not going to let anything happen to him.

This was after the showing of the *JESUS* film. Satan greatly tried to hijack the showing of this powerful film. Many times, drunken people and demon possessed people would come and would cause a great commotion. One night while they were dismantling the screen, projector and generator, the nationals who had seen the film were trying to steal the poles that held the big screen up. They wanted these poles for their traditional beer making. The leaders were able to grab them and none were stolen.

3. Each August, we would have Associational Women's retreats. Most of the women in the villages would participate in these retreats. At one specific retreat, we had three demon-possessed women. They would have terrible fits, almost like an epileptic. But the bad part about one of the women was that she had a baby. In her fits, she would lie on top of the baby and try to kill it. We kept praying and praying and for some reason, the demon would not leave the lady. She kept trying to lie on top of her baby and kill it. We later visited this lady. She was the wife of the leader of the church! She had the little rope amulet, and a rope around her waist that showed she had been to the witch doctor. We went to her house and talked to her and her husband, about how she must cut this off and burn it, to remove the power it had over her. She did burn it, but then when we went back in a few months, she had been back to the witchdoctor and had them again. The leader of the church left this woman, his wife, because she never was healed and she caused great pain.

At these retreats, there was no electricity of course. So when the sun went down, I must say it was frightening to be the only white person for miles around. I had no cell phone and no way to contact anyone if there was any trouble. In the dark, it made these demonic fits more horrible and terrifying for those of us trying to deal with them!

At one of these meetings, I had a very bad feeling. It was in a more remote area, where the people had had little teaching about salvation. During the night, as I was alone in my tent, they sang and chanted and beat the drums for the entire night. But I knew by the style of music, that it was not Christian music, but music for the ancestors. During the night, some teenagers came into the camp where us ladies were. One of the young men knew I was in there, and wanted to do something to me. He urinated on the side of my tent and it came in through the screen. I had a terrible migraine when I got home the next day! Needless to say, I was not eager for August to roll around as I would begin to dread the two nights and three days of camping - because you never knew what was going to happen!

4.   I have already mentioned earlier a place called Lugela. This was the place that Mike wanted to plant a church, but to get there was quite a mission! It was the place where Mike rode in a canoe (with his bike), a taxi, and then when the taxi went no further, he had his bike to finally get there! He found a group of people that wanted to begin a Baptist church, and he found and discipled a potential leader. They needed a plot of ground to build a little church, and they found one near the leader's home. But in the lot was a banana tree that had been planted by the witchdoctor for protection. He refused to move the tree, for fear of what bad things would come to his home if he moved it! The perfect place for the new church was not to be because of the belief that this tree had power!

5.   Many times these evil spirits would be present at a baptism. Many missionaries would tell you about times that when they were baptizing someone, the person would go limp, and even another voice would come out of the person, other than their own. Many times they would resist the baptism and refuse to go under the water. This happened to Mike one time as he was baptizing someone. She immediately went limp and this strange voice began to speak and protest the baptism. Needless to say, the baptism doesn't go on, but prayer for the poor person bothered by the evil spirits.

It would be easy to get very discouraged by converts to Christianity that still practiced their ATR. Instead of dedicating their new baby to the Lord, or their newly planted crops, they would go to the witchdoctor to get protection. We would tell them that God is a jealous God and He doesn't want to share our trust with anyone. Also, teaching them about Jesus and the Holy Spirit, and the direct influence they have on our daily lives, was a much-needed topic to discuss.

We could give you a hundred examples of times we were disappointed by the syncretism. But some Mozambicans would really be converted and refuse to continue in their traditional practices. One such couple was Pastor Gregoria and his wife, Esther. They lived in a very rural place, a long day's trip to the clinic. He would travel to the clinic over dirt roads on his bike. If his wife or child were sick, he would carry them as well on his bike. His wife became pregnant, and it was time to deliver the child. But the labor came too quickly, and by the time he tried to transport his wife, the baby had died during the delivery. Two more babies died in this same way - they did not see the labor signs coming and did not get to the hospital on time.

The family of Pastor Gregoria's wife met and told them that the ancestors were angry with them and that their house was cursed. This was why these deaths were happening. They told him they must move and leave his church, that these things were happening because his house was cursed. He told his in-laws that he was going to pray and trust God to give them a healthy baby. And God honored their trust and stand for Him - the next year, a precious, healthy, baby girl was born to them.

One Final Hardship

We were so excited when we heard that we had new IMB missionaries coming to Mocuba. We had written a job request and had waited for many months for it to be filled. I have already spoken about Sam and Kylah Clark-Goff who filled this request. But we immediately began to worry about where they were going to live. It is up to the missionary that wrote the request to get a place for them to live and completely outfit it with what they will need for the two-year assignment. This was not an easy task due to the inavailibilty of stores and goods! So we went all through Mocuba and found several empty houses for rent. We, ourselves, wanted to move from the present house we were in. The house we were in only had two bedrooms, and Timothy and Grace were getting older and needed their own rooms. So we had decided that we would look for another house to live in, and then they could live in our old house. The house we were living in already had the cistern and had been completely redone, so it was ready. Now we would just have to do all that again to the new place for us. But we had several months to prepare and we got busy!

We found a lovely house that we were interested in. It had the right amount of bedrooms and was very nice and had an extra lot next door that could be used for Mike's demonstration garden. The house was not in good shape, but an Italian man had rented it last and so some of the things, like the plumbing and electricity were fixed. The main problem was that almost all the windows in the house were broken. There were other problems as well, and our Logistic Coordinator (LC) with the IMB came up and spoke to the "owner" of the house. He told him our desire to rent the house, and that these repairs must be done quickly, because the new family was coming. The "owner" agreed to fix the necessary things in the time limit that we had. In the following weeks, we would drive by the house and could see that nothing was being done, and time was running out! The missionary that was serving as our LC contacted the "owner" and he kept making promises. But we were able to tell the LC (who didn't live in our town; he lived two to three days away), that nothing was being done.

We got worried and began to look around for another house to rent. We could have fixed the things ourselves, but the IMB didn't want to rent from a man like this that would lie and was not trustworthy. Something was definitely up, and the IMB didn't want to get in the middle of it! The lies were intense, and things weren't adding up. So we eventually, by the grace of God, found another house to rent. Our LC called the "owner" of the other house, and told him that because he had not kept his end of the deal, that we were, in fact, not going to rent the house. The "owner" of the house verbally threatened the LC, Gil Santhon, saying to him "I know where you live". Our LC lived in Maputo, the capital, and he and the "owner" had talked about Maputo and he did in fact know where our missionary lived. We began to get quite worried for our safety as well. Although the LC is to handle all the legal arrangements like this, we feared for our safety, because we were in the same city as the "owner" – seeing him often when we went to town.

Two days after the "owner" threatened Gil, Gil was mugged and attacked in Maputo. He was coming out of the bank, with a lot of money (remember the exchange rate was 25,000 to $1.00). Since he was the LC, he had to pay the guards at all the mission-owned houses in town, thus had a lot of cash on him. He was robbed and beaten up. When we got this word, we were terrified that this "owner" had done it, or either arranged it. But we have since felt that it was just a "normal" robbery. Many times, in the capital city, they would target people that they had watched get lots of money out at the bank.

In time, we came to find out, the "owner", was not the owner at all! In these post civil war days, and squatters rights, opportunistic Mozambicans just grabbed the nice brick houses which the Portuguese were forced to flee. But many times there were no deeds to the houses, and families would began to fight over who really "owned" the house. So, in fact, we were dealing with an estranged brother of the real owner of the house. He was trying to get the rent money from us, while in fact; the real owner had the only set of keys to the house. We wondered why we never saw the inside of the house! This man we were dealing with had no dibs on the house at all!

For several weeks and even months after that, we didn't let the children ride their bikes alone in the city. We did not know what this crazy man would do!

The difficulties that have mentioned in this chapter are great. Luckily, they didn't all happen at the same time. Yet at any given time, we may have been dealing with several of them. So it was never just one thing that got you down, for instance, living with the heat. It was always that you were dealing with several of them at one time. It was the culmination of several of them put together. So if we are honest, it was a very hard place to live. We constantly had to go back to "our call". We had to remember it, re-evaluate it, and decide to be obedient to this call, or not. When we were out of the situation, like on furlough, I must say it took all the strength we had to leave America again and go back – the first time, we didn't know what we were getting in to, but the second time we did. I actually made a list of why we must go back. Number one on the list, was that "our stuff was there". This sounds very crazy, but we honestly had to think of every reason why we HAD to go back. But it always came back to "our call".

The Plight of the African Women

The past few pages have been about the hardships of our lives in Africa. I must say though, that even though you may read through it and feel it was a very hard place to live, in many ways, we had it made. We had power and water most of the time, and had money to buy food. We knew we could get medical care if we needed it, even if it meant an emergency evacuation by plane. But the people that suffer the most - far superior to anything I have mentioned - are the African women. They suffer more than any people I know. They literally have to do all the work around the house. They have to birth the babies and care for them. Many times they have walked to the hospital to give birth, or they have been driven on the back of an old bicycle. They then have to nurse and care for the children - many times nursing for years due to lack of other food. Having poor nutrition themselves, I don't know how their bodies actually produce any milk. I have seen many a hungry baby, nursing on a flat, empty breast.

Then they must grow all their own food. Their farm would have had to be outside of town. In the small city we lived in, the huts are close together, and there is no land around the houses to grow food. So they would walk for hours out to their farms, and they would do all the hoeing, planting, cultivating, and harvesting. Many times they would stay in little mud huts out on their farms, so as not to have to commute each day. They would have had to save seeds, as they wouldn't be able to buy them. So part of their harvest, would have to be put back and guarded to be next year's seeds. At harvesting time, they would need to pick all the produce, and then transport it back to the city. At times, they would load it, one sack at a time onto the family bike. Then they had to dry all the corn and cassava, and grind it into meal. This they do in a large wooden urn, and then take a huge stick and beat it for hours on end. If they grew rice in the wetlands, they would need to pick it one little grain at a time, and then beat it to take the husk off. A handful of rice was a gift of great value - when you consider that they had harvested each piece and basically pealed each little grain. These women did all the food preparation - from growing, to preparing, to cooking, to washing up.

Then they must go to the river, or to the public tap and draw all the water, carrying it on their heads back to their house. This precious water would need to be used to cook with, and to wash dishes and their bodies. The thing is that this water is not clean, and one would generally not drink it. If they had a husband, they would need to boil water for him so that he could have a hot bath. To do all the cooking and boiling of water, they would need to go and collect firewood, or cut down trees.

Then many times they would walk to the river to wash their clothes and their dishes. The river was so muddy, but that is all they had to wash their clothes and dishes with. Many times, instead of fetching water to bathe at home, they would bathe in the river - but the man had to have his bath at home, and his water had to be hot! Aren't you tired just from thinking of all this?

They would also have the normal chores that most women have - cleaning the house, the yard, and clothing everyone. They would sweep the dirt each morning in the front of their houses. Since they lived in such community, they did this so they could see whose footprints had come to their house that day.

Due to the infant mortality rate, many women had lost a child, and many times more than one. They were no strangers to grief. They would bury their child one day, and be at their farm the next day. They had to survive.

If they were not Christians and were partaking in the traditional, animist ceremonies, they would also have to brew the beer that they would put on the ancestors' graves, and they would be involved in these ceremonies. The women were seen as the keeper of the traditions, and responsible for passing them on to their children.

Many times they would be the second, or third wives of a man. This means that if the man had a small income, he would need to share it with 2-3 women and all the children of these women. (That is another reason the poverty is so great.) So the women would stay with these men even if they weren't good to them, just so that a couple of nights a week, their husband would come home and MAYBE would bring some salt or some soap, or maybe a chicken. Then the other nights during the week, he would be with his other wives, and you couldn't question where he was. He is the boss, and can decide when he wants to come to be with each wife. The women stay with these men because of poverty - with all the work they did in the farms and in the houses, and in drawing water, they were absolutely at the disposal of their husbands to provide a few clothes, or salt or soap. They also, culturally, do not see that they can stand up to their husbands - even if they are beaten or mistreated. They had to take it.

The saddest story that I heard of was something that happened to a woman at Christmas. She had decided to go to church for a Christmas Eve service. Her husband didn't like her going to church, and normally, to obey him, she didn't. But because it was Christmas, she decided to go. She prepared a nice, hot meal for him, but prepared it without salt, as she had no money to buy salt, and he had not been to her house in a long time with provisions. He had been with his other wives. The man killed his wife when she returned from church because his food had no salt. Although this shocked some people in our city, most just said this was nothing unusual to them.

Chapter 13

BLESSINGS AND EVIDENCES OF GOD'S POWER AND GRACE

1. The People of Mozambique

AFTER SUCH a long chapter on the difficulties, let us now turn our attention to all the blessings we experienced while we lived in Mozambique. I think the thing that sticks out in our mind is the way we fell in love with the Mozambican people. When the early explorers landed in what is now Mozambique, they too found them to be very kind and friendly people. They named the country, "The land of the good people."

Soon after we moved to Mozambique, we had to leave the country for the weekend and go get supplies/food in Zimbabwe. We arrived back home late in the afternoon from our trip to Zimbabwe, and after a few hours we heard a knock on the door. It was the night guard – not the one on duty for that week, but the one that was off duty. He had heard that we had made it safely back from Zimbabwe and he had come over to pray with us to thank God for our safety. We were so touched by this – to see their great faith that everything is a gift from God, even traveling mercies, and when we receive a gift, we must say thank you.

Many of them had such a hunger for the Word of God. We had several men that would walk 20 miles to come to the Bible courses. Others would ride their bikes that distance, and even longer to come to our house, or to hear Mike teach. Many times men drove from great distances to ask Mike to please come to their area to

see the new church they had started. They would then need great
training and help.

They always wanted us to visit their churches and to evangelize
and help disciple the people in their villages. For a white missionary
to come by truck to their remote locations was a once in a lifetime
opportunity for them. For us to get to many of these places, the
church would have to cut down trees for our car to pass, build
bridges, and make a small path or road for our car to pass. When
we would finally get to their church after the path had been cut,
the members of the church would line the path cheering, singing,
clapping and dancing. They always had fresh flowers on the mud
pulpit, and had them hanging on a string down the middle of the
mud building. (Most of the time, the flowers on the pulpit were in
the only vases they had - beer cans! After seeing that in church
after church, I decided to get some contact paper and cover the
beer cans so they would have prettier and more appropriate vases!
I gave these to many of the churches.) We always got quite a royal
welcome. I would feel like I was Princess Diana.

Three pastors from Mozambique that lived eight hours from
us showed up at our gate late one night. They had heard there
was a new missionary in Mocuba, and thus we were the closest
missionaries to them. (They were very near the Malawi border,
and there were missionaries actually closer to them, but we were
the closest in Mozambique.) They came to our house to ask Mike
to come and teach TEE (Theological Education by Extension) up
in their area. They were the most dedicated men. They would
ride their bikes all over that area to teach, evangelize, and try to
start churches. They would do it for no pay, and would cover great
distances. Communication was always a problem, and every time
someone came to our gate it was the first we would know about
it. So when we would be locking up for the night, we would hear
someone outside, and many times it was these three men. They
would be hungry and would need a place to sleep, after traveling
on a crowded bus for eight hours on dirt roads. Even if we were
dead tired, I would have to fix them something to eat and be
hospitable! I must say this was another very hard thing - to be so
flexible about who showed up at your gate. You may have made
plans for the day to be with your family or do something else, but
when someone rides up to your gate and they have ridden 40 miles

by bike to see you, you drop what you are doing to give them food and meet with them!

Many other leaders did the same, all over the province where we worked. They loved to show the *JESUS* film to their people. Most of the time, Mike took it in his car and stayed with it. But as we began to trust the people, and they began to know how all the machinery worked, Mike would let them take the equipment on their bikes to the various villages. They could get to places that he could not get to by car. The leaders from the various churches would arrive, 3 at a time, to carry the equipment on the bicycles. One would have the screen, the other the huge generator and the other, the projector. They would sometimes go to ten unreached places to show the film, and it would always come back in perfect shape. We must say the first time we gave out this equipment, worth thousands of dollars; we thought to ourselves that we must be crazy! But we just had a deep sense that it would all be returned, and it was! This is a testimony to the honesty of the Mozambicans, as well as their commitment to reach their community for Christ.

One day I was taking the youth choir from my church to another church to sing. We were trying to encourage this new church start. We also wanted to encourage the youth at the new church to also form a choir. There was a young man in the group named Eusebio. He was a natural leader and helped me with the youth ministry. We were to leave at 9:00, and at 9:00, he was nowhere to be found. We waited and waited, and I asked everyone where Eusebio was. He had never just not shown up before! Someone said that on their way to the church, they had seen him at the market. I was livid and couldn't believe he was shopping when we needed to be leaving - we had a long distance to travel and didn't want to be late for the service! So we loaded everyone up and went to the market. There I saw Eusebio outside the market selling something! I went up to him and said, "what are you doing; did you forget about us going to the new church?" He said that he had to sell his egg first; that he couldn't go to church without an offering. He put me in my place! This is the example of commitment.

They would thank us for coming to visit them each time we came. Mike would come back from a weekend out with a church, and he would always have a truck full of things - huge stalks of bananas with 50-75 bananas, live chickens, rice, eggs, sweet potatoes and other things. Remember, this is one of the poorest places on earth. I will never forget one of those ladies' meetings. At the end of it, all the ladies were told to come up and give me a gift to thank me for coming. They would walk down the center aisle of their mud hut churches and one by one, they would hand me an egg or a potato or other such gifts that they had grown. I will never forget an old lady walking down the aisle and giving me a handful of rice. It wasn't even in a little plastic sack. She had grown the rice herself, picked it grain by grain, and hulled each grain by hand (separating the shell-like hull from the grain). She was so poor, she didn't even have a sack to put it in. What a priceless gift!

Truckload of gifts after a church visit.

One day we went to visit our domestic worker's home, that was working for us at that time. Her house, so sparsely furnished, only had a bamboo mat for a bed, two chairs, plus a metal pipe that she used to build her fire in to cook their food. In her poverty, she went to the field behind her house, pulled off a ripe sugar cane, and cut it in two pieces – she said we must take them to Timothy and Grace as a gift. Talking about the widow's mite – this lady gave all she had to give.

I must add that now we live in Cape Town, South Africa - quite different to Mozambique. We moved from one of the poorest countries in the world to the richest country in Africa. We work among the Xhosa tribe. Although many of them are poor, compared to the Mozambicans, they are very rich. They have public hospitals in every area of our city, and most have running water and electricity. Their roads are paved, and they have schools and libraries in every township. (A township is where the blacks were forced to live during apartheid. They are free to live anywhere they want now, but many still live there.) We have ministered here for almost five years and we go to minister in the townships at least five days a week. We have done many things to meet the spiritual and physical needs of the people here. I must say in the five years time, we have received *one* gift. That was when we left the church we were at during language school, and moved to Cape Town. We had gone to church there for a year, and were then moving very far from their city. They gave us a beautiful ceramic bowl, and gave Mike a barbeque tong set. But that is the only gift we have ever been given. In Mozambique, the poorest of poor would fill our truck with things they sure could have used theirselves. They did this week after week. Mike rarely went anywhere without coming back with a truckload of gifts.

Another thing they would do was write up these official declarations when you had done something for them. They would be in a very official Portuguese, kind of like a resolution made by a convention. Sometimes they would be three pages long. One time we had ministered to the handicapped people in our city. We had a Special Olympics day, with prizes and all. We presented the Gospel afterwards and it was all on the radio. After this day, we were presented with presents, as well as an official declaration. We would get them before we left for furlough, and then when we came back, we got another one. One of the main coaches was trying to learn how to speak English, so he gave the last one to us in English. Here is a short excerpt from one of the declarations we received when we returned from our last furlough (I have left the misspelled words and grammar mistakes on purpose):

In the name of Jesus Christ, our Lord, we greet everybody here. The baseball team want say wellcome to the Boone's family, and thanks God for bringing them back, wholesome, this family that did us great help. They showed us the right way to recognize the Lord Jesus and taught us one of the famous world sport- baseball. We specially once more praise the Lord for the joy He gave us since they arrived.

They were so grateful for our work and presence in their city and lives. We got several of these declarations during our time there, and they are still precious to us!

We would be so amazed at their loyalty to us. We rarely felt afraid. They would rather die than let something happen to a white person in their care. This is illustrated by the fact that when it came time for Mike to baptize in the river, they would always wade out into the river first. This is so that they could see if there were any snakes or crocodiles, and to see the depth of the river. They would find a nice shallow place to stand, one that did not have a huge drop off, yet deep enough to submerge someone. In the 5-½ years, this probably happened 30-40 times, and each time they would wade out there first!

Mike baptizing a new convert in the local river.

2. The other missionaries

Not only did we have the love and support of the Mozambican people, but we also had many friendships with the other missionaries. We too were like family, as we shared the same calling and many of the same difficulties. We were very fortunate to have so many missionaries in Mocuba. At one of our Sunday night English fellowship groups, we had a pilot from South Africa visiting. He had flown up some things for some of the missionaries and had stayed with us for a few days before flying home. We were so grateful for that room under our split-level house. We didn't keep a guest book, but we should have! We had so many people, from so many different countries, stay with us on their travels through Mocuba. Mocuba was on the main road from Malawi to the north of Mozambique, so if people had gone to Malawi to the doctor, for vacation, or just to get supplies, they always had to pass our home. Since we had no phones for several of those years, we never knew when they were coming. Some would only arrive at 10:00 or 11:00 at night, as they had been stuck on the muddy roads. But missionaries from other cities and other guests knew they would always find a clean bed at the Boone guesthouse!

As we were sitting in that service in our home that Sunday night, the pilot gave a testimony. He was weeping as he was talking. He told about how, during the war in Mozambique, he would try to fly in supplies, but he was always shot at. He had always prayed that the war would end and that one day missionaries would be welcome in Mozambique and that they would be able to lead many to Christ. As he sat in our living room, with the 30 other missionaries, he was so aware that God had answered his prayers. It was a very touching moment for all of us to realize our presence there was an answer to many faithful prayers prayed years before.

Just as well as experiencing the loyalty of the Mozambican people, we too felt loved and honored by our colleagues. We would all celebrate birthdays together. When you live in a city with nothing to do, a one-year old's birthday party is cause to get together and have a party! Because there was no TV station, or video shop, we would go to each other's homes and borrow videos. We seemed to have the most, and at times, I felt like I was working at Blockbusters, but usually I was happy to loan them out. When one family got a satellite disk, they would invite us over to watch the Olympics, and even taped them for us to view the next day.

I will never forget the love we received when the September 11 tragedy happened. We were the only Americans in town. But some friends of ours had a satellite dish. They were watching TV when the breaking news came on about the planes that had just crashed into the towers. I was busy home schooling that morning when I heard someone at the gate. It was this missionary and she told us that we had to come immediately to her house to see what was on TV. She was crying and just kept saying, "America has been attacked, America has been attacked." Now she was a South African, married to a French Canadian, but she felt such pain for us as Americans. I will never forget the outpouring of love that we received from people - from the other missionaries, and the Mozambicans. They were all so supportive and concerned. It was like we had been personally attacked.

Many times the missionary fellowship would need to step in in times of sickness. One family would have some medicine that the other needed, and you knew that they would help you out. One time, I got very sick. I was loosing weight, and had terrible diarrhea and stomach cramps. We only had an Italian doctor in our town, and she had given me some medicine, but after a month, I was really in bad shape. (With the Italian doctor, I always wondered if she understood what I was saying- her Portuguese was terrible, and she didn't speak English!) The other missionaries were very concerned about me and offered to help. They knew that Mike traveled a lot and that I was home alone many times. One of the missionaries from the Netherlands told me that even if I needed to go to Malawi to the hospital in the middle of the night, he would take me! He said that I could call on him at midnight and we would pack up and go - and one knows you never travel in Mozambique at night! (The hospital was from 5-7 hours on a terrible dirt road - depending on whether it was rainy season or not). Fortunately, in a few days, another Dutch missionary was going to Malawi, and they took me to the hospital. The love and support was incredible. We depended on each other so much.

We had a single young missionary man from Papua New Guinea and he also was very susceptible to malaria. He was in the Mocuba hospital several times. We would take him some good homecooked food and visit him and pray with him. But one time that he was in there, several of the men in his room had died of malaria in front of him. He was really depressed about being in this dingy place and really began to feel he was going to die also. Malaria is a terrible disease and you feel like you want to die! We tried to talk to the hospital about releasing him, because he was so low emotionally, that we were very worried about him. We had a nurse in our English fellowship and she had agreed that if the hospital would release him, she would help nurse him back to health in our home. Well the doctor refused to release him because he told us he was in critical care. We were convinced that part of the problem was the condition of that hospital and the surroundings. So we went into the hospital and kidnapped this young man, sneaked out the side door, loaded him in our car and brought him to our house. I had brought IV's with me from the states. A missionary nurse in our English fellowship came over every few hours to change his IV's. We were up all night the first night staying with him; just monitoring his critical situation. We brought him a TV and played movies for him, and turned our window AC on. In just no time, he was healed. But we were convinced that had we left him in the hospital, he would have died! Needless to say, our pastor, a nurse at the hospital, was very angry with us about that, but we felt we had to do it. It was a matter of life and death. Plus, I had more medicine and supplies at my home than the whole hospital put together!

I have already mentioned how we all supported each other in teaching the many MK's in town. We all took turns one afternoon a week teaching recorder, art, music, drama, Christian interpretive dance, etc.

Many of these missionaries and even one national from Mozambique have come to Cape Town to see us in our new assignment. These are life-long friendships, formed through a mutual sense of need and through Christian service.

3.   Blessings in day-to-day life

Although generally life was quite hard, God would always bring special surprises. I can remember going to the market and trying to find some fresh fruits or vegetables to have for our family. During certain months of the year, there was nothing but tomatoes, garlic and onions. It would be the end of the season, and there was just nothing. I was so discouraged and prayed for God to help me creatively find things to feed my family. About that time, someone rang our doorbell. A young teenage boy was selling cucumbers that he had gotten in Malawi! We hadn't seen a cucumber in a long time! It was so wonderful to eat that cucumber and be able to tell the children about how God had provided it. It was the best tasting cucumber ever!

Other times when there would be nothing at the market, I would go to some of the little Asian shops. They would often drive down to South Africa to get goods to sell in their shops. But, by the time they made it back to Mocuba, many things were not good any more. But on this one day, I went in to the shop and a man had cantaloupe! Again, that was the best testing cantaloupe ever! Another time he had grapes and strawberries. Again, they had come by road on the four-day trip to South Africa – so they were pretty special.

Another day, the kids and I were quite bored. There was a little ice cream stand in town that we would go to. The only thing is that many times they had no ice cream! It, too, would come from South Africa, and sometimes in rainy season, people didn't make that four-day trip. So if they didn't have ice cream, we could still get a nice, cold Coke in a glass bottle - the best tasting kind. One day, I was particularly down, and we decided to ride our bikes to the ice cream shop. To my surprise, there was a ping-pong table on the front lawn of the little shop! I couldn't believe my eyes! We played for several hours. The next day, we went back to play again, and it was gone. I went back many more times, and it was never there. I begin to wonder if we had really played ping-pong, or if I was going crazy and we really hadn't! Maybe it had been a mirage. I mean, why would someone put it out for one day, especially since everyone was enjoying it and they could make money off it?! So I asked the owner about the table, to see if maybe I could buy it. He took me into his house and showed me the table. It had been played so much on the first day, and it was in such bad shape to start with, he had had to put it up and get it repaired. I never saw it again. It was things like this that God would do, just in the nick of time.

Another time, we looked out, and our neighbors across the street had opened up a little stall. We went over there to see what they were selling, and they too had ice cream! The kids and I couldn't believe it. Again, it lasted just a few weeks, until the ice cream ran out, but we grew to really appreciate the little surprises from God.

Pets also helped to bring joy to our day-to-day life. In the course of our time there, we had a pig, rabbits, cats, dogs, fish, birds, chickens, and even a baby duiker - a little orphaned antelope. When Mike was out in a rural area visiting a church, a man in the church had the antelope for sale. The mother of the duiker had been killed and a hunter brought it to the church and had it "for sale". Mike bought it for about $2.00 (50,000 mts.) Many times the bigger deer were hunted, and then the babies were left orphaned. Mike brought her home and we began to bottle feed her. It would follow us around the house and loved to suck on one's ear! It lived for many months. Unfortunately, we had a trip planned to Malawi and had to leave it. We showed our workers, who were there 24/7, how to care for the duiker and prepare the bottle. But while we were gone, she died. We don't know exactly what happened, but there were two very sad little MK's when we got home!

Mike experimented with a rabbit project to hopefully teach the people how they could raise them at home, and thus have more meat for their families. We tried not to give the rabbits' names - as one gets quite attached to them when they have names! Grace loved to pick them up- but one time she dropped one. I then heard her and her little friend next door praying for it to be healed and not die. It didn't!

There are many 'dog stories' - when one was stolen, the next day, another one just showed up! There were no vets for the first 4 years that we lived there. But God provided in that a woman that lived in Mocuba, and worked for a non-governmental organization (NGO), had trained as a vet in Nigeria. She was able to come over and give advice when we had sick animals. One time our dog was hit by a car, and with the use of medicine for people, and the help of this lady, our dog was nursed back to health.

Precious puppy and new baby

In Mocuba, there was a small airstrip. Most of the time, the airstrip was used as a thoroughfare for the people to walk and ride their bikes. But about once a week, a little plane would land. Everyone would be so excited when they heard the plane overhead. The pilots had to circle the strip over and over to get the people to get off the airstrip. Then as soon as it would land, the airplane would be swarmed by onlookers. You would think the people that got out of the plane were celebrities being attacked by the press. Occasionally, people would take advantage of an airplane that was already coming to Mocuba for another reason, to send us supplies. Missionaries in Zimbabwe would offer to buy items for us and send them. What a blessing to go to the little airstrip and get boxes of powdered milk, coffee, ketchup, even meat. Talk about service!

4. Holidays and Birthdays

Holidays and birthdays also helped to alleviate the boredom and give us things to look forward to. At each birthday, we prayed and tried to make it a very special time for the kids. You really had to be creative when resources were so limited! One year, when Grace was five, we went to this hotel and had her birthday on the Seventh floor. In this war-torn country, it was so amazing what was left from colonial days. This hotel, one could tell, had been beautiful in its time. The elevator still worked and there was a beautiful marble spiraling staircase that was also there. I made her a Barbie cake - where you put the body of the Barbie in the middle of the cake, and then make the cake her large dress. But in February, one of the hottest months, the cake melted and all the icing ran off the cake, and there stood a naked Barbie in the middle!

Another year, we found this old horse farm in the city where we had language school. There were still a few horses and we had Timothy's party there. Each child got to go for a short ride around the ring and that was such a treat. The place also had a disco, with a very large sound system, and they said we could bring whatever tapes we wanted to and they would play music that the children would like over the system. So we had Veggie

Tales and Alan Jackson playing and Timothy thought that was great!

Since the 4ᵗʰ of July is an American holiday, we generally celebrated it by ourselves, since we were the only Americans in Mocuba at that time. One year on the 4ᵗʰ of July, Timothy lit some firecrackers off in our yard. The Commander of the Army came over to our house in just a few seconds and wanted to know what that sound was. He was very angry and thought we were shooting ammunition. After 20 years of war, he was of course concerned. Needless to say, we never did that again!

We celebrated other holidays in a traditional way. Christmas is not a big deal in Mozambique. The once Communist government took it off the calendar and replaced it with Family Day. We would always tell the people that it was *Family Day* - the celebration of the Holy Family: Mary, Joseph and the baby Jesus. We never though got use to Christmas being at one of the hottest times of the year.

Christmas Day could be a very depressing day, but we would try to have people over and make it a cheerful day. We would always have the English fellowship at our house, and one Christmas day, we had people from 14 different countries in our living room. We each sang Christmas songs from our country and as the different carols were sung in the different languages, there were not too many dry eyes in the place. We had Christmas carols from Brazil, Burundi, Nigeria, Holland, Germany, Kenya, Papua New Guinea, South Africa, America, Mozambique, Finland, Sri Lanka and others. We also each brought dishes from our own country, and it was very interesting to taste the different dishes. After they all sang, that is when we went outside and saw that most beautiful double rainbow. "The heavens display the Glory of God; the skies proclaim the work of His hands. Day after day they pour forth speech. Night after night they display knowledge. There is no speech or language where their voice is not heard. Their voice goes out into all the earth, their words to the end of the world. " (Psalm 19:1-4a) We felt we were at the end of the world, but He was there! He truly did come at Christmas to be the Savior of the whole World!

Here is another of our friend Kylah's poems that really summarizes my views on Christmas in Mozambique:

In the Month of December

In the month of December, our thoughts turn to things above
With mangers and carols and gifts for those we love.

We just love the Christmas season - preparing hearts and homes as well
A time for family and celebrating - as His story we re-tell.

In living Christmas tree, nativities, and carols we proclaim:
"To this world was sent a Savior, and Jesus is His name!"

But there is much of the world that knows nothing of these things—
So they don't celebrate the birth of our King.

They can't celebrate- because they have never heard
The story of Christmas, of salvation come to earth.

God's Son and our Savior who was born in Bethlehem—
The most precious, perfect gift that has ever been given.

The light of the world and the hope of all mankind
But unaware of that light or gift, they are so very blind.

Here in Mozambique many folks could not recall
Ever hearing "Good news of great joy shall be for ALL."

There are no Christmas lights, no decorations anywhere
No nativities or caroler - it's incredibly bare.

Because the light of the world they haven't yet viewed
And the song of salvation is an unknown tune.

So in this month of December, let's also turn our thoughts
To all of those around the world who never have been taught.

Through prayer and missions studies and with your offerings
Through your service there at home or maybe traveling.

You are light to the world and good news to "ALL" you bring
So they too can celebrate the birth of the King.

Thanksgiving, of course, is an America tradition, so we would generally celebrate that in Quelimane where more Americans lived. There would be some non-Americans and it would always be fun to tell them what Thanksgiving was and how it got started. A real tricky thing each year was to try and find a turkey to cook. One year, a pilot was coming around October from South Africa to bring other supplies and we thought ahead and asked him to fly us up a turkey! He kept it frozen and it was such a treat! Another year, we found a farm outside our town that raised turkeys and pigs. We went out and bought the fattest turkey we could find and we brought him home. When we asked our house worker to kill him so I could cook him, he told me that he couldn't, that the turkey didn't have enough meat on him. He looked pretty big to us, but what do we know about live turkeys? So we told our worker that we had to have a turkey - that we were having a get together with many other Americans and I was responsible for bringing the meat! So he agreed, but he was right! There was hardly any meat to cook. I did cook what little meat he did give me, but it was the nastiest tasting stuff you have ever eaten! So we had chicken for Thanksgiving that year!

Here is another wonderful poem from Kylah, about Thanksgiving.

Thanksgiving in Africa

It's Thanksgiving in Africa - whatever does that mean?
The skies are growing cloudy and for rains we are hoping.

The temperature is 105, give or take a few,
It's difficult to even picture, the fall that we once knew.

For in this land of Africa, things are not the same.
The temperature's all backwards and the landscape is all changed!

Instead of leaves and pumpkins, scattered all around
The mango trees are bursting and we find them on the ground.

The calendar says "November" but it doesn't quite compute.

We choose shorts and capulanas. Jean and sweaters won't quite do.

There's no Friday night football, and basketball they will not play.
I haven't run with mom to Sliger's for decoration of pumpkins and hay.

Dinner with all the family, we won't make this time
But all of that home-cookin' is etched into our minds!

Temperatures, environment, and tradition all may change.
It's Thanksgiving in Africa, and everything is strange.

Everything except one thing may be different or odd,
But the very meaning of this time's the same: We thank our God.

We're thankful here in Africa, even if it isn't fall.
We're thankful for when games played here, are with a soccer ball.

We're thankful for the sunshine, for the mangoes, for the warmth.
We're thankful for electricity, running water, occasional storms.

We're thankful for plenty to eat and drink, for God's call unto this land;
For colleagues and companions here who truly understand.

We thank God for you, our families. We just can't say enough
How we appreciate your encouragement, compassion and your love.

Thanks for all those e-mails and the calls that make our days.
With grateful hearts we thank the Lord and give Him all the praise.

Because it's Thanksgiving in Africa, whatever that does mean.
It means we'll count our blessings, and to God our thanks we'll bring.

5.   What a blessing trips, vacations and visitors were!

Each year, we would have an annual missionary meeting and then at another time of the year, we would have our annual prayer retreat. All the missionaries from all over Mozambique and the country of Malawi would gather together for these meetings. Once every several years, we would have a big meeting with all the missionaries from about ten different countries. Also, once every five years, we would have a Ladies Retreat and it would also be for the missionaries in the neighboring ten countries. And all missionaries in their first term, go to a First Termers conference and this was a big help because you have so many unique issues you are facing in that first term.

At each of these meetings, a team from America would come to help with these and would always lead the missionary children in a Vacation Bible School. Each team would come solely for the purpose of ministering to us all and encouraging us. They would bring American treats and food and really spoil us all. We really can't underestimate how much these trips away helped. It gave Timothy and Grace the privilege of going through a normal, American VBS curriculum, with all the crafts and Bible studies, songs and games. They would usually get a shirt with the name of the VBS theme on it, and they still treasure these T-shirts - each with a special memory! It always amazed me how these teams from the states would spend two to three thousand dollars apiece to come to Africa, just to teach the MK's. Sure, they would get to do some sightseeing, but basically, they would pay with their own money to come and lead a VBS. You know how hard it is to get VBS workers in the states - imagine telling someone that to teach, **they** had to pay between two to three thousand dollars! So you can imagine that the people that were willing to take vacation time and spend that kind of money were the cream of the crop from the churches back home.

The adults would also generally be led by the pastor of the group of volunteers from the states. We benefitted greatly from each of these times of spiritual growth. The setting of the meetings was always beautiful. Most of the time we met on Lake Malawi - the fourth biggest lake in Africa. Its beauty is breath taking. It was so big that one could easily feel you were at the ocean; it had a beach and waves and it stretched on forever! The resort had an Olympic-size pool, a Jacuzzi, trampoline, playground, an aquarium, monkeys, boating, and many other amenities. Of course, at each retreat, we were required to go to many meetings and, just like business meetings at churches, some of these meetings were stressful and controversial. But, generally, the setting, the team from the states and the fellowship with the other missionaries far outweighed the stress of the business that took place.

Each time we heard a team was coming from America, we would ask my Mom to mail them things that they could bring to us. We depended on these visitors to bring us many needed things. They would bring us our bank statements, medicine refills and important items like Kool-aid packets. We are forever grateful to everyone who came to Africa to minister to us and for all the things they would bring. And it was wonderful that they could then take back gifts to our family. One time we had visitors from America that came in August, and I sent back Christmas gifts for all our families. I knew that was the last chance I would have to send gifts to them. You had to always think ahead and send gifts whenever you got the chance – even if it was months ahead.

As well as these annual meetings, we as a family would take time away. It was a blessing in that we could drive to Malawi, Zimbabwe or South Africa for holidays. The traveling time and the roads were definitely challenging, and at times, we wondered if it was really worth it to drive for 4 days to go on a vacation! But we really did see some marvelous things in the course of our years in Mozambique. Before Zimbabwe began to fall apart politically, it was a wonderful place to visit. We loved the animal parks, the national parks and the botanical gardens. We went on so many safaris, even letting Timothy ride an elephant. There were times to feed baby rhinos and to learn about animals. We have seen so many beautiful African animals! And the food in Zimbabwe was really something to brag about. As I look back, these trips really refreshed us and allowed us time to reflect and gather strength for the months ahead.

Mike and Timothy riding the elephant in Zimbabwe

On one of these trips, we were at a game park in Malawi. It was built right on a river and the river was full of hippos. At night, the hippos would come out of the water and they were all outside our tent. We heard them - they were so loud! Well, in the middle of the night, I had to go to the toilet, and the bathhouse was a little distance. I knew the hippos were outside our tent, but I had no other choice! I thought to myself, how dangerous can a hippo be, since they have a campsite right on the river where the hippos live! So I went to the bathhouse and passed many hippos on the way. I found out later that hippos kill more people in Africa than any other animal! They are extremely dangerous, especially if they are guarding their young!

Although we could buy some things in our city and in the city two hours away, each time we went to Malawi or Zimbabwe or South Africa, we would stock up on groceries. We had a huge freezer and refrigerator, because we would stock up for three to four months at a time. So crossing all these borders was always scary, because we would be loaded down. So, although it was a blessing to travel, the borders and the challenges on the road did take a lot of the pleasure out. But, we learned so much and our horizons were broadened at each journey!

6. Spiritual Growth of the Children

I will conclude this section on blessings, by saying how much of a blessing it was for our children to grow up in Mozambique. I would not have wished for them to live anywhere else. They were so protected and their lives were so rich and full. Both accepted Christ at one of these missionary meetings. Timothy was baptized on Easter Sunday in our home church in Mocuba. He was in the first group of people that were baptized in the new building. Generally, they would go to the river for their baptisms. But they so wanted an indoor baptistry, so they included that in the building plans. Timothy was one of the first ones to be baptized inside.

Before they baptize anyone, they call the candidates to the front of the church, and they ask them questions. They have been through a baptismal class, and before they baptize them, they want to make sure that they really know the Lord and the doctrines of the faith. So Timothy stood up in the front in a long line of 12 others that were to be baptized. Because of the ancestor worship and traditional African beliefs, they felt obligated as a church to make sure that the person really understood what it meant to be a Christian. Many times, people would want to be baptized, thinking that this, along with their traditional beliefs, would make sure they would go to heaven. So they were quite strict on who they baptized. So it was a good practice to ask the candidates some questions. If they didn't pass the "test", they wouldn't be baptized! So many were quite nervous, including Timothy! Because Timothy wasn't perfect in the language, Mike stood up there with him and when the pastor asked a question, Mike translated it for Timothy. Then Timothy would answer in English, and Mike would then answer in Portuguese to the pastor. Well, Timothy was getting all the answers correct, but the pastor was concerned that maybe Mike was telling him the answers. Since none of them knew English, they didn't know if Mike was helping him or not. So in the middle of the "test", the pastor told Mike that he thought he was helping Timothy and he turned around and asked if anyone else spoke English in the church that could translate for Timothy and would not be tempted to "help" Tim. So fortunately, a young man named Bruno, that did speak good English, came forward. He then carried on helping Timothy with the test.

After the pastor asked the questions that they had been over in their baptismal candidate class, he would open the floor up for the people in the church to ask questions. This was really a very silly thing to do, because sometimes the people in the church would want to trick the candidates. They would ask very difficult questions, like Bible trivia, that had nothing to do with salvation! The pastor would not stop it either - it was like they all tried to ask the most difficult question, just to show how much they knew personally. So for instance, they would ask, "Who was the mother of Moses?" Well, I agree that is good to know, but not necessary for salvation! So we began to dread every baptismal service, because the church just got a kick out of tormenting these new candidates! Fortunately, Timothy passed the "test", and Mike was able to then lead him into the pool and baptize him. All the fellow missionaries had come to celebrate this time with us, and it was a marvelous day and a precious memory.

Timothy's baptism

As I have said, growing up in Mozambique was a wonderful thing for Timothy and Grace. When people in the states felt sorry for them because they didn't have all the trappings that America had, I just knew that if they could see their lives, they would not feel sorry any more. It was kind of like growing up in the 1950's. We had no TV, just some movies. For many years, we had no phone. We lived in a small town and would walk or ride our bikes everywhere. We were rarely in the car - maybe Timothy and Grace would go somewhere one time a week. They played outside constantly and climbed trees and were not in front of a computer or TV. They had friends of all ages, and learned to speak to adults. They would appreciate the smallest thing, like getting an ice cream cone. We had so much family time. They were educated with the finest home schooling materials that had a Christian worldview behind it. They learned to serve and participate in the ministry with us. They learned another culture and some language. They saw poverty firsthand and hopefully will always remember how blessed they are - and that we are blessed so that we can then share.

It was wonderful for the children to be involved in ministry. When we would visit the churches in the outlying areas, we would always take crayons and coloring pictures for the children – so the kids would have something to do during the four hour service! It was Grace and Timothy's job to pass the crayons and paper out.

When we passed them out, at times the children did not know what to do with them. Some of the children were ten years old and had never colored. So Timothy and Grace had to demonstrate, while the children would stare at them.

On Easter Sunday one year, Mike had been asked to preach at a local church. They ushered all four of us on to the raised little mud stage that they had made. The church was packed. All the children of the church were sitting on grass mats at the front of the church. It just worked out that Timothy and Grace were on the stage right in front of about 70+ kids that were staring at them – watching their every move. They were very good at first, but as the service wore on, Timothy and Grace were bored stiff. So they decided to be a clown in front of the kids. They began to make funny faces at the kids, cross their eyes, and then even stuck their finger up their noses. The children were just dying laughing. Tim and Grace made a F- as a MK that day!

But, I must admit at times I really felt sorry for Timothy and Grace. I knew as rich as their lives were in Africa, they did miss out on many things - mainly relationships with their extended family. They grew up missing out on so many family occasions and those crucial relationships with grandparents and extended family. Plus the benefits of a good church with all the programs for children, and a school!

One Sunday, we were riding our bikes to church. It was over 100 degrees and there had been no rain. Everything was so dry and dead - like living in a desert. There was no grass or flowers or anything of beauty. (This is one of the first things we would notice when we would go to Malawi or Zimbabwe - they had grass!) Everything was so dusty. A layer of dust would settle on everything in the house and you couldn't get rid of it. It would just come right back. We were on our bikes and I was looking at the town that we called home. I was thinking how sorry I felt for them to have to grow up in a place like this. The roads were dirt and the houses were not painted. I felt so sorry for making them go to a four-hour church service, where they would understand very little of what was going on. They would have Sunday School, if the teacher showed up. (She came about 50% of the time). Sunday School would just be a lady telling a story under a tree. There were no crafts or anything fun. Generally it was okay when it was not 100 degrees, but that day it would be unbearable.

I was thinking of how sorry I felt for them when Grace looked at me and said, "Mom, I am so lucky to live in Africa. I get to see such beautiful things, and most children in America will never get to see the beautiful things that I get to see. Africa is such a cool experience." Those were her exact words, and I had not fed them to her, because I hadn't told her how lucky she was in a very long time! I had been down and feeling sorry for our family. I learned so much from my daughter that day! Beauty really is all around you; we must just find it. From that day on, I tried to find one thing of beauty each day.

Chapter 14

OUR WORK IN MOZAMBIQUE

AFTER READING our story and hearing about the 28 cases of malaria and the 10 robberies and the two accidents, one may wonder why we did not want to leave - even when we were told to by our sending agency. It is because of this: the call of God on our lives and the work that gave us such great satisfaction. In the course of the book, I have alluded to a lot of different things we did, but I thought I would mention other things as well.

Theological Education by Extension- TEE

Theological Education by Extension was Mike's main job, along with the agriculture ministry. This gave him such fulfillment because he was training people that would not have another chance to go to a seminary. So he went to them and gave them a basic Bible degree without them having to leave their home, families and churches. There were many books that they would have to complete, and it was in three levels: basic, median, and advanced. In 10 different locations, Mike had over 120 students. It was such a joy to hear the testimonies of these church leaders. One man came and told Mike that, as a result of the course, he did not beat his wife anymore! This was a common practice, yet the Spirit of God convicted this man as a result of a study on Christian marriage!

The JESUS film

It was also a huge joy for Mike to oversee the translation of the JESUS film into Lomwe, which was the African language where we lived. (It was already in 1049 other languages in the world!) This was a major project with very strict regulations on how it must be translated. It had to be done by a committee represented by all the major denominations in the city - so it was a blessing to get to know the Catholic priest and pastors and leaders from other denominations. The translation had to be done, and then tested out many times to see if it was understandable by all. Then the voice actors had to be found and hired that could do every character in the film. After many months, they went to the recording studio and taped it. When the film was finished, a premiere was planned. Visitors from the states that had helped to finance the translation came, and a huge reception was given for the government officials in Mocuba after they saw the film. The Campus Crusade group that came from the states estimated that there were between three and four thousand people to view the film. They said, that to date, this was the largest premiere of a film in a newly translated language. God greatly used this film as Mike showed it literally hundreds of times. There is no telling how many people will be in heaven because of this film!

Church Planting and Agriculture

I have already mentioned that Mike was responsible for church planting in the Lowme part of our province. He would travel to the different churches and areas, and train and evangelize. Many times he would baptize on Sundays at the conclusion of a time of evangelism.

He would also always use this as a time to teach against ancestor worship. At one new church plant all the children were wearing amulets around their waists. They were given these by the witch doctor when they were born, so that they would be healthy and protected from the bad spirits. After a time of commmitment and a prayer for protection, all the mothers brought their children to the front to have these amulets removed. They were then burned as this signified they were putting their complete trust in God.

As far as the agriculture side of his ministry, he had a demonstration garden plot next to our house where he experimented with the crops that he would help the people with. He would then invite pastors and leaders and other church members over to the house to see the farm, and he would explain how they could do the same. Therefore, he always had to do it just the way they could do it. He couldn't use expensive fertilizer and chemicals on his that they then could not afford. His demonstration farm was the talk of the town! Even though it was organic, they would always think his farm looked so good because he had "white man medicine".

Mike took advice from another agricultural evangelist: that the job there in Mozambique would really be learn-as-you-go. He told him that all the knowledge that he had learned in America, at home and at the university, would really be of little help! The growing seasons, crop varieties, soil, rains, etc. were all so different, that he would have to experiment at home with what works. Mike spent hours each day experimenting with different growing schemes and plant varieties. Remember, there would be no way to water the crops. So everything had to depend on the annual rains. At times, these came too late, and the people lost all their precious saved seeds. Other times, we had flooding and the crops were lost. And to a totally agrarian society, if their crops failed, the situation was hopeless, as they didn't have money to buy their food. Mike, in the six-year period that we lived there, became a wealth of knowledge. This was another reason why we didn't understand why God would have it in His will for us to leave. All that Mike learned in Mozambique would be of little help in South Africa, as then again, all the factors in agriculture change from country to country, as well as the cultural differences.

Due to so much hunger, the goal was to help each Mozambican to have a better yield in their harvest and food security. Mike studied carefully and did many tests on how close together to put the plants. The Mozambicans had always been taught that the corn must be planted very far apart, so that each plant could get enough sun and soil. But they ended up having lots of wasted space that could have been planted and it would result in more food!

He also raised rabbits at home, and the plan was to distribute mating pairs to the different pastors and church leaders, so they would have meat at home. But the climate was too hot and the rabbits wouldn't mate. He built the rabbit pens out of bamboo and other local materials that they could then copy. Then he built it in such a way as to collect the droppings. This would then be turned into manure for the garden. His plan was to teach all this, but the rabbits didn't multiply as he had hoped.

He also had a goat project. He divided our area into agricultural associations. Each association received ten goats. When these produced nine females, these were to be given to another association.

An additional male was supplied by Mike. The plan was for this to continue to every association in our province.

He also had church community gardens where he would help them to produce extra food for their members. He tried to develop agricultural co-ops so that they could have a market in which to sell the food. He also did a seed and hoe distribution many times in many different areas. He taught them how to save their seeds and showed them how to improve the quality and growing power of the soil by doing crop rotation. He found plants and flowering plants that would act as natural insecticides, because there were no chemicals that the people could afford to buy. He also taught composting as a means to enrich the soil. He introduced a new variety of sweet potatoes that contained more vitamins. They were used to growing the sweet potatoes that are beige or light brown. He introduced the orange variety, and they grew wonderfully there! He saw many truckloads of these nice, healthy potatoes that they had never heard of until he came! In many ways he was like an agricultural consultant, or extension agent - all with the purpose of reaching people for Christ through it, as well as meeting their great physical needs.

Meeting Physical Needs

I have already mentioned how our home was our office and how we daily received knocks at the gate from people in need. They knew they could come to our house for Bibles, medicine, food, literature, glasses, use our copier, etc. Sometimes we would get as many as ten visitors a day. Sometimes it was easy to see these as "interruptions". Each one had to be offered drink, and since they are relationship oriented, you had to find out about their whole family and what was happening with them at the time! In our Western mindset, we would just want to hand them what they came for and let them be on their way. But we had to see that they were God's plan for that day. They weren't "interruptions" but "divine appointments."

They came for many reasons. Many times they would just come to bring us a gift and invite Mike to come to their village. It would always be such a blessing to hear them ask for glasses. They would always say, "I just want to be able to read the Bible again." Other times, people would come to the gate to borrow the wedding dresses. We were always thrilled when this happened, as this would lead to a time when we could sit down and visit the couple and do some pre-marital counseling. (I have already mentioned that most people just lived together, because they would never be able to pay the enormous fee that the government required for a civil wedding.)

Another blessing was being able to get wheelchairs for the handicapped. It was not uncommon to see grown men unable to walk, crawling on their hands and knees. My father went to the large Catholic Cathedral one Sunday just to see it, and each person would file up to the front to receive communion. He told us about a man that couldn't walk that crawled up to the front to receive communion. In one of our Baptist churches, there was a young man named João that was participating in the courses that Mike taught. He would come to the church from his house, on his hands and knees. He would get old plastic flip-flops, and he would put them on his hands and knees to give him a little cushion as he walked. We were able to secure a wheelchair for him, and there are no words to describe the joy that was on his face when he received it. The wheelchairs were hand-cranked and could be driven by those whose legs were paralyzed or crippled from birth, or from land mines.

We had just presented this wheelchair to João.

Modelling a Christian Marriage and Home

Mike and I always felt that one of our main ministries was to just model for people what it meant to have a Christian marriage and family. One day, we were outside talking to a church leader who had come to visit. The man asked Mike a question about when he could come to their church for a possible visit. Mike then turned to me, because I generally have a good idea of future dates, and Mike was unsure of our plans. The man immediately asked Mike why he was consulting his wife. He said, " You listen to Amy?" To them, it was not normal for a husband and wife to have a discussion - what the man says is what would happen. Through this, we realized that they were watching every move we made and every word we said! It made us very conscious not to have a disagreement in public! Many times in the TEE classes, marriage came up and Mike would always try to share with them how important it is to have family discussions and also a friendship with your wife.

Construction of First Baptist Church of Mocuba

We were also very involved in the First Baptist Church of Mocuba. The construction of their new building was a major work, because Mike ended up providing the transportation, being the contractor and the controller of the money. The last Sunday we were in Mozambique, they dedicated the beautiful new building to the Lord. It was a very special ending to our years there.

the old church building- Before...

new building- After

Starting the English Fellowship

I have already mentioned how special the English fellowship that met at our house was. We invited anyone and everyone that either spoke English, or wanted to. When one of the missionaries had a ministry teaching English, the fellowship was a wonderful way for them to work on improving their English. On any given night, we would have people from 15 different countries in our living room. What was so special is that the people that came were from all different denominations and mission sending agencies. It was really a picture of the Body of Christ - we had Catholics, charismatics, and people from the reformed church in Holland, for example. It was great practice for spending eternity in heaven with saints from every race, culture and nation (Rev. 5:9).

One day, our family was playing badminton in our yard. A man stopped us and asked us, in English, who we were and where we came from. (We stood out because we were white!) We told him about ourselves and then asked him about his life. He was from Sri Lanka, and had just fled there due to the violence in his country. He belonged to one of the small sects that they were trying to annihilate. We invited him to play badminton, and he had been a badminton player in Sri Lanka! We also invited him to the English Fellowship. He came every Sunday night for a year, and then, wanting to get refugee status, went to South Africa. We wrote many letters for him to the United Nations High Commission for Refugees (UNHCR) to try to help him get refugee status.

Another day, we heard that there was a white woman selling things at the market. This was a first! We wanted to find out who she was and her story. Come to find out, she was an American that had come to Mozambique to work for some NGO agency. She had fallen in love with a Mozambican and they were now married and had a child. But the husband began to drink and he would beat her regularly. Her contract had run out, and the husband was unemployed, and there she was selling boxes of juice in a grass-thatched little hut in the dusty market. We invited her to come to the English fellowship and she just seemed to come alive during those worship times. We would pray with her when she would arrive with bruises on her face. She came over often after she had been beaten, and other times we visited her in her home. Fortunately, her parents in America came to her aid, after they realized the danger she was in, and they paid for her to go home with her baby. I often thought of how she would have coped, had she not have had this English fellowship.

Intercessory Prayer

As our numbers grew in the English fellowship, we began to feel like God wanted us to unite as an intercessory force - really praying for the betterment of our city. As a group, we watched the Transformation videos that show how this united prayer force has literally transformed many cities in the world. We planned several prayer walks, and each member of the fellowship combined with Mozambican Christians, and we covered the city in prayer. The question we asked all the prayer walkers was, if Jesus lived here in Mocuba, what would He see? We must see the world through His eyes, and the things that break His heart, must break ours.

We had enough people that we could break into 10 groups, and each group had eight places to walk and pray in front of. We prayed at all the bars and taverns, the hospital, at the Mosque, at the police station and jail, the schools, and government offices. We prayed in front of the witchdoctor's house and at each church - especially those that taught false doctrine. We prayed at the town park where there was a lot of prostitution. We prayed for every ministry that was represented - for example, World Vision, Trans World Radio, and the English classes. The town looked like a ghost town, in that many buildings were empty because of the poverty and the war. We prayed in front of every empty shop that soon people would have jobs - since most are unemployed. We prayed for the city water department, as the pumps and other equipment were very old and constantly breaking, meaning we were sometimes without water for days. We prayed in front of the administrator's palace (like the mayor). We prayed for the roads as we walked over huge pot holes that literally could swallow cars and prohibited development.

We then began to pray one afternoon a month - specifically for the problems in the city. Soon after we began this united effort, we saw miracles happen in our city. A large, noisy bar on the main road, that was operating and open all night long, was an area of concern. Our hearts were grieved as we stood outside that bar and saw mothers with babies on their backs, getting drunk, and staggering out in the main road. But praise God, it closed down almost immediately!

We were very concerned about the education in town. The main public schools left much to be desired, as the children sat on the floor and did not have textbooks. We therefore prayed for desks and books to be supplied. One day, soon after our united prayer effort, we were standing outside, when we saw a huge 16-wheeler truck pass our house with hundreds of school desks! We had specifically prayed for desks to be provided by the government, and in just a few weeks, there they were!

Another great concern was the hospital. It was in such a horrible state. There were no trained doctors, and very little medicine. If you went to the hospital, all they would give you would be aspirin or the medicine for malaria. Whatever illness you went in there with, those were the two medicines you would get! And many people have so many other dangerous, tropical illnesses. The corruption was terrible. When the government would send up medicine, it was stolen by the workers in the hospital, and sold at the local market. We went to the hospital, as a group, and walked around the premises - from the TB ward, to the pediatric ward, to the morgue. We prayed for God to really work in that place, and transform it from the inside out. Soon after we prayed, we began to see many foreigners from Italy in town. They were working for a company that had come to completely revamp the hospital buildings. Windows were put in, where there once was broken glass. Screens were put up to keep the mosquitoes out, and even ceiling fans were put in to help with the terrible heat. New beds were bought and the buildings were painted. In time, a new doctor came, and he was a Christian - also a member of our fellowship. We began to support him through prayer and God used him to change that place around. I still would not want to be a patient there, but it was a hundred times better than it was! "The effectual, fervent prayer of a righteous man, availeth much."! (James 5:16)

Prison Ministry

Near our home was one of the Mozambican prisons. It is difficult to describe the horrid conditions. I can't think of many worst places in the world than an African prison. It was a square cement block of buildings with a courtyard in the middle. Only one meal a day of very meager means was provided. If you did not have family to bring you food and water, it would be very difficult to live there year after year. Everyday, there would be a huge line of family members outside the prison, bringing food. My heart always broke for those that were just visiting Mocuba when they were arrested, and didn't have family locally. They, therefore, would only get the one meal of mush a day. I have already mentioned how there was no water at the prison, and how one year we took barrels of clean, cold water on Christmas day to the prisoners. Some of the people in the prison were real offenders and dangerous people. Other times, due to the corruption, innocent people were thrown in there. There was a serious lack of lawyers and court officials, so inmates could stay in there for years before their case would come up. Most of the time, to get out of prison, it required a huge bribe to the judge, and most of these men had no money. From time to time, different youth in my youth Sunday School class were in there for minor things, or they had been framed.

A very valuable ministry we did with the prisoners was the Bible Way Correspondence Course. I have already mentioned that it is a course that consisted of ten books. The prisoner would study and read the book and the Bible verses, and then they would take a test of that material. I would then grade it, and if they passed, they would get the next book. After studying all ten books, they would have a very good understanding of Christianity, as the course included all the key aspects: the Ten Commandments, the Gospel of Mark, Christian marriage, etc. I would go to the prison and give out the first book to all the new prisoners that weren't there the week before. Then I would collect all the exams that they had completed in the past week since I had been. In the 5-½ years that we were there, hundreds of men and women participated in this program. After completing the ten books, I would go and present them with certificates, and they would treasure these certificates - sometimes it would be the only possession they had.

We also had a worship service and sang with the prisoners each week. It was a blessing to take along some of the youth from the First Baptist Church with me, and to expose them to this type of ministry. If nothing else, I am sure it made them want to never do anything to be put in there! The person that helped me the most in the prison ministry was Raul. He walked with a crutch, and one of his legs was terribly deformed. He would ride his bike to my house - yes, ride a bike with one leg! We would then go to the prison together, and many times he would preach to the prisoners. I loved to see Raul's Bible - almost every page had some writing or verses highlighted. You could see he loved the Lord and His Word.

Teaching People to Read and Write

I taught literacy under the gazebo in our yard. One of the ways to determine how advanced a society is, is to see how many of its people can read - the literacy rate. When we lived in Mozambique, the literacy rate was about 33%. So many people would come to us and ask us to teach them to read; they so wanted to read the Bible. So, I began to meet with ladies in our church that wanted to read two afternoons a week. I would also train other teachers in the other cities that we were responsible for, so that this work would have far-reaching effects. I would then visit the classes, check up on their progress, and present certificates for those that completed the course.

It was such a blessing to see the women after they had learned to read. They would proudly carry their Bibles to church, and volunteer to be the one to read the Scriptures aloud. One time we were at a wedding. At the wedding, the bride and groom must sign the marriage license. We observed the bride taking a long time to write her name. When she finished, she looked up and grinned, and said that she had just learned to write her name in the literacy course. She was smiling from ear to ear.

There was another part to this story too. Sometimes during class, I would have to go inside for a few minutes to attend to the kids, use the toilet, or turn on the washing machine, etc. While I was inside and not looking, the ladies would always go over to our demonstration farm and steal a few things for their supper! I would see all kinds of things stuffed in their shirts or wrap-around skirts. The main thing they loved to eat was pumpkin leaves - and we weren't going to eat those anyway, so I just gave the leaves to them. But we literally had to stop having the class in our yard because of the theft. And these were ladies from the church; one was the charter member! But to them, it wasn't stealing, because we had so much and we should share! I tried to explain that they must ask first, and then if they do, we were happy to share.

Teaching literacy in a Mozambican church.

Music Ministry

Music was always an integral part of my ministry. I would get so concerned at the church services because many times we just sang the same few choruses and hymns each Sunday. Some of the songs were not even good songs to be sung in a worship service - they would sing traditional songs, or songs they had sung during the war. Many times the songs they sung had no spiritual value - for instance, one time they sang a song about marching through the Promised Land. They repeated the song over and over - sometimes one song could last 10 minutes - and all it said was that they were marching in the Promised Land! I wanted them to be aware of what they were singing and to see the meaning of it, and not just go through the motions.

I did many things to try to help in the music ministry. First of all, I needed to learn a lot of Portuguese hymns and choruses. They did have a hymnbook, but didn't know many of the songs. So I learned them and then would teach them at the Ladies' meeting on Saturday, hoping that they would then want to sing them on the following Sunday. Every Sunday, the woman would march in from the back of the church and they would sing three songs. Because they didn't have any Portuguese music available to them, they would many times sing the same songs over and over. So, as I began to teach them new songs, their presentation on Sundays was more meaningful. I also taught new songs to my youth S.S. Class. I would invite church members over to the house, and we would sing the new hymns with my piano. They loved to hear the piano, since they didn't have one.

Over the years that we lived there, I also began to write down the oral songs that I would hear, as we traveled to the 100 different churches. I would then run those pages off, and wherever I would go, I would pass these song sheets out and teach them to the people. Because none of the songs were written down, and because no one could read music, the songs were passed on orally. Before I left, I had the dream of recording 50 of these key worship songs on a tape, and giving it to each of the churches. I taught all 50 of these songs to a small choir, and we went to the recording studio of TransWorld Radio, and we recorded the songs. We got wind-up tape players that don't require batteries for each of the churches, and they were each given a tape of the new songs, plus the tape player. I continue to pray for God to greatly use that tape.

Mike also ministered in this way. Beside Portuguese, the colonial language, each person spoke their mother tongue. The people in our area spoke Lomwe. It was wonderful when they could sing in Lomwe, because this was the language of their heart. There was a hymnal in Lomwe. Mostly it was translated hymns from English. So written above the Lomwe hymns, they would have the tune name. For instance, the book would say, "sing this hymn to the tune of 'What a friend we have in Jesus.'" The Mozambicans wouldn't know the tunes, so Mike would teach it to them. He couldn't speak the language, but since the language was phonetical, he could sing it for them. They loved learning new songs and through this, they also learned much theology.

Baseball Ministry

One of the best things I did while I was there was to begin a baseball ministry. Mocuba had a shortage of school buildings, so the children would go to school in four-hour shifts. There was always a huge number of children and teenagers roaming the streets, since they were only in school for a short time each day. There were also no extra curricular activities for the children, like sports in the afternoon. They literally had nothing to do. I began to hear about the exciting baseball ministry in Zimbabwe that was run by one of our missionaries. I invited him and a team to come to Mocuba to introduce baseball. He also was very involved in wheelchair basketball for the handicapped in Zimbabwe. So he brought a few disabled guys to also demonstrate that.

So for a week, we showed up at the soccer stadium downtown, and begin to have baseball clinics. In the afternoon, we went to the handicapped center, and showed them the wheelchair basketball demonstration. But we began to realize that the poverty in Mozambique would never allow for us to be able to buy the expensive wheelchairs needed for wheelchair basketball. Many disabled didn't even have a regular wheelchair, let alone a second wheelchair for sports! So we showed them how to do other sporting activities - like wheelchair relays and games like that. At the end of the week, we gathered all the people together and had a baseball game, followed by relays for the handicapped. Then we had one of the handicapped men from Zimbabwe share his testimony. When a person is handicapped, it is always thought that that person was cursed by the ancestors. Most of the time, they feel that they are not fit to live, and in many cases, handicapped babies would be starved and allowed to die. So this Zimbabwean man was able to tell them that God had a purpose in creating them this way, and that they were not cursed, but rather blessed by God. This program was on the radio, and we heard that God greatly used this man's testimony to reach many of the disabled that heard it. Due to the landmines, it was very common to see people with one leg or one arm. Also, due to the primitive hospitals, many had birth defects that could easily have been fixed in a more developed country. So this was definitely a message that needed to be talked about.

After this week, we had a long list of people that wanted to play baseball. I tried to quickly train some coaches, but everyone was learning about the game for the very first time! They had never heard of baseball before, and really thought it was a game that I had made up! Many times after a game, the players would come up to me and thank me for making up such a nice game! I would tell them that it was a huge sport in the world, and that many people made big bucks playing in the big leagues, but they had never heard of it before! So one night, I invited all the players over and I showed them a video tape of the World Series. They loved it and this helped them see it was a real game in the world!

It was very special that Timothy played in the ministry and the other missionary kids as well. The other missionary boys from Holland and South Africa didn't know baseball either. So it was quite a treat to see the three little white faces among the many Mozambican players.

At first, many of them would kick the baseball, like in soccer. It became such a problem, that we had to tell them that if they kicked it, they would have to sit out and let someone else play! It didn't help that we always had to play on soccer fields, since of course, they had no other types of fields.

After the leagues began, we started to take the game out to the more rural areas from Mocuba. We were told by the missionary in Zimbabwe that it was best to not play with gloves, but rather to play with a soft baseball, called an Incredi-Ball®. This way, the game could spread rapidly to the outlying areas, and all they would need would be a ball and bat, and not all the gloves, which might be difficult to provide if it really spread. Since the people were really not used to playing organized sports, it was always so interesting to see what the people would wear to come to the baseball clinic. When visitors came to your town, it was customary to dress in the nicest thing you had. At times, ladies would wear lacy nightgowns, because they thought they were prettier than their plain dresses! (They bought all their clothes at the used clothes market). One day, at a baseball clinic, a guy turned up in 1960 polyester dress pants (from the leisure suit days), and a dress shirt with the collar turned up. Then he had on these pointed white leather shoes with a big heel - again from 1960. We nicknamed him Elvis as he tried to play this newfound sport in his nicest clothes!

The ministry did really grow and became the primary ministry I did, beside homeschooling my children. There were hundreds of young boys that were ministered to through baseball. Many were Muslims and most unchurched. After we played several games and had practice, we would always gather under a tree, and I would give a Bible study. Many of them also took the Bible Way Correspondence Course if I saw that they were really eager. I also formed a choir out of the oldest baseball players, and we traveled with this choir to different churches, the prison, and did small concerts at different events. Many of the baseball team would come to the Sunday Night English fellowship, and were even given turns in preaching and leading the music. It was a wonderful discipleship ministry for them.

Churches in the states would collect baseballs, bats, and bases for us and in time, we did collect gloves and use them. Another thing that the churches donated was old baseball trophies. So at the close of each year, we would have a tournament and then present the trophies. You would have thought I had given out pure gold! I started by giving the trophies to the team captain, but it got to be such a problem that people would try to steal the trophies from the captain's houses. So it was sad, but I actually had to present the trophy, and then take it back, because it was presenting too many problems for the captains. It was also a blessing to show the *JESUS* film after these tournaments. One time we showed it in the big soccer stadium and over 2,000 people were there.

I will always be grateful to the First Baptist Church of Madisonville for sending a group of volunteers to help in the baseball ministry. It was a huge boost to our program and many were saved as a result of it. I am also indebted to Celestino Pempe, a Mozambican that was my right hand man in the baseball ministry. He worked with those boys and also shared with them spiritually, and really had a vision of reaching them for Christ.

In many ways, to keep the game simple, we had to modify the rules. For instance, we didn't allow stealing the bases, because it was just too many rules at once. But after time, I told them about stealing the bases. I didn't realize what a stir this would cause! They just couldn't believe that a missionary was telling them to "steal". They thought it must be a bad thing, and they didn't want to do it! We actually had to rename it to something else, because they took such offense at being told to "steal"!

I had such a love for my baseball guys. In many ways, we all became family. I took them on a picnic on the top of a mountain, and was always having special things for the winners of the games. They were so appreciative of me and this ministry. Sports evangelism is a wonderful ministry, and will open doors, almost anywhere.

Members of Timothy's baseball team, after a tournament.

CONCLUSION

I MUST SAY that we are so thankful to have lived in Mozambique for the time that God allowed us to. We learned life lessons, and we will never be the same. It was such a blessing to have learned to live by faith. It is so easy in our modern culture, to not have to *really* trust in God. When we need medicine, we just go to the pharmacy. When we need a doctor, there is a wide choice of them for us to choose from. When we need glasses, we just go to the optometrist. But we had no choice, but to put our complete hope in God and trust in Him to act and do the impossible - in life and death situations. But even if you live in a very modern city with all the conveniences and advanced health care, He is still the Great Physician and worthy to be consulted and trusted.

During the time we were in Mozambique, we would always pray before we left for a trip - even if it was a small trip. We knew of the dangers and knew of our need of God's help. When we moved to South Africa, and the roads were better, and we had cell phones, I found that we stopped praying before each trip. The Lord spoke to me clearly: I was trusting in the good roads and cell phones, rather than the Lord. Still to this day, if we are driving out of our driveway, even if we are going on a trip that is just for one hour, we stop and pray for God's protection and for His angels to accompany us. Our hope is not in reliable, new vehicles, cell phones, or Triple A emergency services. Basically, if we don't pray, we are in essence saying to God that we don't need Him. Our hope must be in the Lord!

I want to be like the man I met back in Nigeria in 1984 that prayed for God to give him glasses. I don't want to just go to the optometrist without even praying or thinking about it. I want to pray for that doctor to make a correct prescription, and then I want to pray that God will help me to get the best glasses. I don't want to live my life being so content with all the pleasures around me that I totally don't need Him. We needed Him for our very survival, and I still want to live each day like that.

If given the chance to do it again, I would do it all again – even knowing now what I do, I would do it again. The malaria, the robberies and the two accidents involving pedestrians - I would do it again. I am so glad that today I can be thankful for all we went through. I can be grateful because I was able to see God's hand through and in it all.

Many people ask how Mike is doing after having so much malaria. What the doctors told us is that probably his liver would be damaged from so much malaria and medicine. But he was checked soon after leaving Mozambique and his liver is normal. This is another miracle of God. He does have bad headaches, which could be caused by having had malaria so much. But since we are not in a malarial area, he is not exposed to it, and will not have any new side effects or cases. We praise God for His healing power.

> Our family theme verse for our years in Mozambique was:
> "The Lord will guide you always;
> He will satisfy your needs in a sun-scorched land
> And will strengthen your frame.
> You will be like a well-watered garden,
> Like a spring whose waters never fail." Isaiah 58:11

We did live in a sun-scorched land, but we saw God provide for our needs. He did guide us and did strengthen our frame. We didn't always feel like a well-watered garden, but we knew that the spring we were watered by would never fail. We can testify that His word is true.

What has God done for you? Have you forgotten any of His benefits? If people don't say thank you for the things, events and people in their lives, it could be that they feel they are "self-made men". That is a very sad saying that we have. There is no such thing as a "self-made man." So if one doesn't say thank you, is it because they feel that they earned it by their own strength? Also, if one doesn't say thank you for the good and the bad, it could be that they don't believe that God allows us to go through difficulties, and that He is sovereign over all things. I encourage you to start a little journal called a "Forget not all His benefits book." Daily write in the journal all the things that you are thankful for. Doing this can sure help with depression.

To Him be all praise and glory for everything that we were able to do. Our thanks to the many people who walked the road with us and prayed for us. We very much felt the prayers of the saints, and it was such an honor to be prayed for. Right before we left for Africa, I heard the Ricky Skaggs song, "Somebody's Praying". When times were tough, I would recount the words in my head:

Somebody's praying
I can feel it
Somebody's praying for me
Mighty hands are guiding me
To protect me from what I can't see
Lord I believe, Lord I believe,
Somebody's praying for me.

Angels are watching
I can feel them
Angels are watching over me
There's many miles ahead 'till I get home
Still I'm safely kept before Your throne
Lord I believe, Lord I believe,
Angels are watching over me.

Well, I've walked the barren wilderness
Where my pillow was a stone
And I've been through the darkest caverns
Where no light has ever shone
Still I went on 'cause there was someone
Who was down on their knees

And Lord I thank you for those people
Praying all this for me.

We did feel that the hands of the Lord were protecting us from things that we couldn't see. And we felt the very angels of God.

This is my Book of Remembrance. May you be inspired to go wherever God calls you, knowing that God will meet all your needs. I pray I never forget what God has done for me.

"God *tries* our faith,
so that we may try
His faithfulness."
- Anonymous